NATIONAL EDUCATION.

NATIONAL EDUCATION.

THE DUTY OF ENGLAND

IN REGARD TO, THE

MORAL AND INTELLECTUAL ELEVATION OF THE POOR AND WORKING CLASSES.

TEACHING OR TRAINING?

BY DAVID STOW,

HONORARY SECRETARY TO THE GLASGOW FREE NORMAL
SEMINARY, AND AUTHOR OF " MORAL TRAINING,"
" THE TRAINING SYSTEM," &c.

LONDON:

J. HATCHARD AND SON, 187, PICCADILLY.
AND SOLD BY ALL BOOKSELLERS.
1847.

NATIONAL EDUCATION.

I HAVE no intention of either condemning, or of giving unqualified approbation to, the educational measure of the Committee of Council, which has now received the sanction of Parliament. But we think that every individual who approves of the State lending its paternal aid towards the moral and intellectual improvement of the poor and working classes (who cannot, or at least will not elevate themselves), will naturally hail with delight the opportunity presented by this legislative measure for putting forth his utmost energies to render it available.

We are disposed to acknowledge the serious difficulties with which the Government has had to contend, in settling this momentous question.

The earnest friends of religious education in the Church of England, the Wesleyans and other Protestant Dissenters, will surely make some appropriate personal sacrifice, to raise their countrymen from their present degraded state of igno-

B

rance, and to render the high-minded people of England also a truly christian one.

We have always advocated large Government grants for the moral and intellectual training of the young,* knowing that otherwise the people would never educate themselves, and that the private subscriptions of the wealthy would fail in providing the requisite funds for that purpose. Let all good men of every truly christian sect and party now heartily unite in the effort of rendering the people of this nation, not merely the greatest but the best—the most moral—the most intelligent—the most pious in the world. Let our strength lie not only in our fleets and armies and mechanical power, but in an intelligent, a moral, a religious and therefore a prosperous and happy people. Let us shew to Government that we can realise all the money it requires of us; and by the prudence of the expenditure lay claim to further and much larger sums.

My object is to shew that while great improvements have been made in Education of late years, still the wants and condition of the people are not yet met by a system fitted to elevate them morally and intellectually, and more particularly to meet the condition of the youth of large towns.

It has been my endeavour for thirty years to work out and present *in practice such* a system, which continues in full operation, and to establish

* See Appendix A. " Moral Training." Edition 1834.

and extend the system at home and abroad, in which about 1200 persons, male and female, have already been trained, besides the many thousands of children who have received the benefits of its natural, christian, and moral training.

Before entering into particulars I shall take the liberty of making a few general remarks.

Almost all letters, speeches, and pamphlets on the subject of EDUCATION refer to the quantity and variety of subjects to be taught, and the kind of books to be used, whether Scriptural, Elementary, or Scientific—the size of School houses, amount of fees, &c. and whether to be taught by monitors or by masters;—but never touch upon *the mode of communication*, (the most essential point after all,) or whether moral results can be produced by other than *direct* moral means.

I shall therefore take the liberty of throwing out in these pages, as a small contribution to my fellow countrymen, the result of a somewhat lengthened experience in the moral and intellectual training of the young—earnestly desiring that the adoption of the principles presented may, by the blessing of God, greatly promote the work of youthful cultivation. We trust also that this may serve as at least *one mode* or system (which has been already triumphantly successful) until one more simple, more natural, and therefore more efficient, is presented by the innumerable host of Educationalists, who have entered the field since we first attempted to form a system for the moral training of the youth of large towns.

Answers to the great question which appears on the title page have filled many a volume, and have been the theme of our most accomplished orators on the platform, at the bar, and in the senate; and yet it must be acknowledged that the whole expositions separately and combined have not proved so satisfactory or so explicit as to receive universal approval. All seem to agree in prescribing EDUCATION as a cure for the evils of society, and yet we scarcely meet with two persons who agree as to what education actually is, or what is meant by the term. It seems to mean anything and everything.

A child is said by some to be *educated* when he can read words of two or three syllables—better no doubt when he can pronounce every word of a sentence, although he may not understand the meaning of one half of its terms, and repeats sounds from memory without attaching any idea to them. He is no more than *educated*, say others, when he can write, cast accounts, repeat the rules of English grammar and knows a little geography; and is simply *educated*, others still declare, when he has passed the whole curriculum of the highest University. What Education is has yet to be defined. In these days *the most important of all the questions we can determine is*, WHAT IS POPULAR EDUCATION? WHAT OUGHT IT TO BE? The wealthy may choose for themselves; they may be satisfied at any step, from the " ab-eb-ib-ob-ub " of the old rote system of the English school, to that which embraces the most finished education. The idea however is now becoming more and more prevalent that, in the true sense of the word, we are never educated—that Education progresses or ought to progress through life—and that, although Methusaleh himself had lived to complete 970 instead of 969 years his education would only then have been finished.

What the education is that will best enable a man to educate himself ought surely to be the sovereign question. Is it *Instruction*, or is it *Training?*---Is it the amount of elementary knowledge communicated, or is it the exercise of mind required by which the pupil may educate himself? 'Till lately the term used to define Education was INSTRUCTION. Give religious instruction, it was and is still said, and this will be sufficient.—Teach the poor to read the Bible, and forthwith you will make them holy, happy, and good citizens,—good parents,—obedient children,—kind and compassionate,—honorable in their dealings,—and crime will diminish. Hundreds of thousands have received such an education—are such the results? We trow not. Have we hit upon the right kind of education, *or the proper mode of communication?* Will all the instruction it is possible to give produce the results which are so fondly anticipated? Will all the *telling* or teaching or instruction in the world enable a person to make a shoe, construct a machine, ride, write or paint, without *training*— that is without *doing?* Will the *knowledge* of religious truth make a good man without the practice of it. The boy may repeat most correctly and even understand in a general way the precepts, "Avenge not yourselves but rather give place unto wrath," "Render not evil for evil," "Be courteous;" but see him at play among his companions, neither better nor perhaps worse than himself, unsuperintended and his conduct unreviewed by parent or schoolmaster, and what do these scriptural injunctions avail him when engaged in a quarrel?—Reason is dormant, passion reigns for the time, and the repeated exercise of such propensities strengthens the disposition, and eventually forms evil *habits*. The father cannot be with his child to train him, whatever his business or profession may be, during the day, and a healthy boy will not be tied to the apron strings of his mother—out he will go, and out he gets to the streets to be with such companions as he can pick up.

In Education as hitherto conducted in school, even under the most highly intellectual system, we have had instruction and not training.— Schools are not so constructed as to enable the child to be superintended—the master has not the opportunity of training, except under the *unnatural* restraint of a covered school-room, and it is imagined, or at least stated, that children are morally trained without their being placed in circumstances where their moral dispositions and habits may be developed and cultivated ; as if it were possible to train a bird to fly in a cage, or a race horse to run in a stable.

Man is not all head—all feeling—or all animal energy. He is a compound being, and must be trained as such ; and the varied powers of mind and of body, although distinct, so act and re-act upon each other that it is difficult to say where the influence of the one begins and that of the other ends. The intellectual to a certain extent influences the physical, and *vice versa,* while the moral influences both and is influenced by both in return. The most influential and successful mode of cultivating the child is therefore when his whole powers are daily and *simultaneously* exercised, and no injury can arise to his varied powers of body and mind, provided they be fed and not stuffed, trained and not merely instructed.

How do we purpose morally, physically and intellectually to elevate the mass of our population, among whom there is not on the part of parents either the opportunity or the intelligence to accomplish this object? If done at all it must be almost exclusively performed by the school trainer. *It is not now done by the Schoolmaster, and it cannot be accomplished by the Parent.* Therefore our youth are growing up untrained, in a moral and even in an intellectual point of view, although it is announced that " the schoolmaster is abroad." In reality we have much said and little done. The truth is forced upon our attention that, *teaching is not training.**

* It must ever be borne in mind then—and would that it could be written in letters of light, over the door of every

What a school for moral and intellectual training ought to be is not yet generally known, or at least is not apprehended. The schoolmaster himself is untrained, or if trained he is not provided with the platform, the sort of accommodation on which he can practise his art, and thus mould and train his tender and important charge. It is not enough "to teach the young idea how to shoot," he must also train, prune and water. And how can he labour without proper instruments—how accomplish his end if practically ignorant of the art? If he must train the "child" he must do more than merely exercise the memory, or the understanding, *or the whole head*—he must cultivate by exercise *the whole man*, in his physical, intellectual, and moral habits—in his thoughts, affections, and outward conduct; and this cannot possibly be accomplished within the walls of an ordinary school room. What suitable school premises for popular education ought to be therefore, remains quite as undefined as the term education itself. The two ideas are in fact inseparable. School accommodation to teach or instruct the head may be just what it has hitherto been, viz :—the one school-room, not unfrequently *dingy, dirty, and airless*. What a school for "training" the "child" according to the rule of scripture *must be*, is quite another thing. The physical, intellectual, and moral propensities and habits, must have *free* exercise under a pro-

educational establishment !—that Teaching is not Training.
—Mrs. Ellis' *"Prevention rather than Cure."*

per superintendence, and the opportunity of development in *real* life—freely at play. We do not speak of jealous watchfulness, or of a system of hateful and hated espionage, but of one where the natural dispositions of children have free scope, and their youthful and joyous feelings have full vent. To effect this, however, there must be the Training School premises and there must be the Trained Master.

After closely remarking the deep moral degradation of great masses of the population in the city and suburbs of Glasgow, and in other large towns in Great Britain, and the effects which education, such as it was, had on their moral and intellectual condition—observing also the actual amount of influence which the sabbath school system seemed to possess in every district of that city—opportunities of doing which, my office as Secretary to its local sabbath schools in the year 1816 and subsequently, abundantly afforded me,* I became fully convinced that our parochial and private English schools elevated the mass of the population but slightly in an intellectual point of view, and their moral improvement under such *Teaching* was scarcely perceptible. In fact the educated, as they were termed, and the uneducated were alike vicious, rude and degraded. Moreover the fact was forced upon my attention, that no suitable machinery whatever

* See "Bible Training, a manual for Sabbath School Teachers." 8th ed.

had been provided, or was in operation to meet the overwhelming power of THE SYMPATHY OF NUMBERS in the comparatively novel state of society, produced by our large towns, in which large masses of human beings are congregated together—the influence of this sympathy being naturally and uniformly on the side of evil. The Sabbath school was, and still is, too weak and powerless to contend with the *sympathy of numbers,* there being, even when best conducted, only the *teaching* of one day, set against the *training* of an opposite tendency during the other six days of the week. In the Sabbath school there was the teaching of the master *without sympathy,* set against the sympathy and training of the streets, and frequently even of the family. Need we wonder then, that the one day's teaching or instruction was (and still continues to be) overborne and counteracted by the six days' *training.*

Labourers,—mechanics,—masons,—joiners,—factory workers, &c. having families may send their children to an elementary school, in which they may be taught to read the bible; but in which from the want of suitable school accommodation, and the nature of the system pursued, they cannot be trained to practise what is therein enjoined.

The children must play in the streets with such companions as they may happen to meet with, and they mutually train each other in the way they should *not* go.

The most pious and intelligent parent finds it

difficult if not impossible to have his children morally trained, however highly intellectual or religious the teaching may be, during that portion of the day when he cannot be with them himself, and although he *could* always be with them himself, they would not be so perfectly trained with him alone, as they may be with a number of companions together, and under the superintendence of a properly qualified school trainer, who might occasionlly join in their sports, and review their conduct after play; and thus not merely put a wholesome restraint upon the young, but act the part of one who would present their varied conduct intellectually and sympathetically in the light of truth and of scripture.

A few words on two or three points of the Training system.

MORAL TRAINING.—By moral training we mean moral *doing*, or the reducing of moral precepts and principles into practice.

In education, school and domestic, the FORCE OF HABIT has never received one tenth of the attention it deserves, not merely in relation to the outward *acts*, but in the acts of thought and affection. As it is in the ordinary intercourse and business of the world, that true Christianity exhibits itself most perfectly in the man; so it is during play with companions, which is the real life of the child, and when learning the rudiments of knowledge in school, that his character and dispositions are most perfectly developed.

It is then that moral training can be more easily and certainly conducted, and a direction given to the thoughts, affections, and outward habits.

It is true even of many respectable men and women that although they have the intellectual knowledge of truth, they have never been trained to, and therefore never practise it. What then may we expect from those, who, although they may have read a little scripture in school, are yet totally devoid of any religious impressions, and have been *let alone to do as they listed,* from infancy to manhood, in the midst of ungodliness, and vice, and crime. This is the actual state of society in this country, and particularly in towns, for want of moral training in school and in the family*—and while school is not complete without family training, neither is family train‐ing complete without that of the school, which possesses the powerfully *operative* principle, of the *Sympathy of numbers.* The one prepares the child more particularly for the domestic, and the other for the social duties of life, whilst as a whole, both united " train up the child in the way he should go."

If it be objected that parents do not and cannot train their children—then the moral training school is the best nursery for exercising those who will become the parental trainers of a future generation, and then by their co-operation

* See Appendix B. " Factory Statistics."

with the schoolmaster will render his efforts vastly more efficient. Christianity may thus be more thoroughly diffused, and the moral sensibilities more highly elevated.

SECULAR TRAINING GALLERY LESSONS.—There can be no moral training which is not at the same time intellectual. We cannot morally train a horse or a dog for example, neither can we reason with them—although the latter from the mere force of instinct, in faithfulness, and kindness, and forbearance under injuries, may well put to shame many who are highly gifted with both intellectual and moral faculties. *Is there no need here for training?* and if the force of *habit* in right or wrong is strong and obdurate, is there not a call to do so *early?*

We must pass through the understanding or intellect, it will be confessed, in religious and moral training, and the same process of *picturing out* and *doing* the thing, whether the act be one of thought or feeling, or physical movement, is precisely the same process by which every subject, whether literary, scientific, or what is termed *elementary in education*, may be best communicated to the pupil—by which in fact he can be best *trained.* The intellectual department of a school education therefore is best conducted on the principle of PICTURING OUT, and by simultaneous as well as individual answers in every branch and in every subject.

The elements of science, natural history, and mechanics as accomplishments, and particularly as applicable to the arts, have been much neglected in school education. Indeed, few have ever acquired much knowledge in these departments in the elementary school, and the consequence is, that scientific terms are seldom understood by persons who in after life listen to the lectures of learned men. Practical men and mechanics no doubt acquire a knowledge of their particular art during their apprenticeship, but how greatly would they be assisted by a previous school training? A regular and daily course of secular training gallery lessons on the picturing out principle, therefore, was established nearly twenty years ago, when juvenile as well as infant departments were arranged in the normal seminary. These training lessons are conducted chiefly *orally*, and not merely from the reading of a book or a list of questions and answers set in regular order. Books on science and natural history may be and are indeed read in our model schools, but the master must be prepared to infuse ten times the amount of information during the lesson to what can possibly be afforded by the daily reading of any elementary book, drawing also upon what little knowledge the children may be found to have formerly obtained. Thus, the bible and daily secular training lessons are conducted on one and the same principle, and each has its own practical use in fitting for the present and future state of our existence. Secular knowledge may even be an assistance to Bible knowledge. Many of the passages of scripture are obscure until we have attained a certain acquaintance with science and natural things, as we may notice in a single paragraph.

BIBLE TRAINING GALLERY LESSONS.—These with praise and prayer occupy the first hour of the day. The innumerable variety of emblems and illustrative points of Scripture when clearly *pictured out*, and therefore made present to the "mind's eye," prepare hearers to understand and appreciate in some measure those allusions made use of in the public service of the Sanctuary, and in the private reading of the Scriptures—not to speak of the direct intellectual culture the analysis of them induces. Public worship scarcely affords time to picture out to the uncultivated mind many of the innumerable natural emblems that might be quoted. The school, therefore, may become a handmaid and a nursery for the sanctuary, by its secular as well as Bible training lessons. Why do the large proportion of an ordinary congregation sit so listlessly under the most accomplished preacher, if not that their minds have not been so exercised, and their knowledge of scripture terms and allusions is so limited that the application and authoritative preaching of the Word fall upon their ears as if expressed in a foreign tongue.

SEPARATION OF THE SEXES.

It will be admitted that a proper conduct between the sexes is of the highest importance, and that unless they are trained together in school and at play for at least some portion of the day, this part of moral training must be defective. Keeping this in view, therefore, we place boys and girls in the *same classes*, with the exception of those more strictly devoted to feminine education, and also in the same play-ground. The moral results are strikingly beneficial: although in the same play-ground, the sexes uniformly play by themselves, and choose their own games, still the fact of being permitted to be together annihilates those fancies which are so much feared ; and whilst the boys animate the girls intellectually, the softening influence of the girls upon the manners and habits of the boys is as strikingly apparent. *

SYMPATHY OF NUMBERS.

This is a principle which has been very much overlooked in popular education.† It is paramount in the assembly, whether Church, political, civil, or domestic. Who has not felt the cheering influence of numbers ? Thinly-filled benches chill the energies of the speaker—the hearers are scarcely less affected. An orator can scarcely rise into enthusiasm whilst haranguing only half

* See Appendix C.

† From Mrs. Ellis's new work, " Prevention better than Cure."

a dozen from the hustings or the platform. Young and old feel the power of sympathy, and numbers together make each individual feel himself personally strengthened. A number of persons, young or old, together, will sometimes do a thing which would cause any one of them individually to shudder. Why not in early life direct this principle to what is right, as well as leave it to itself to produce what is wrong.

The sympathy of numbers, when left alone uniformly tends to evil. It is not surprising, therefore, that large towns without the application of any suitable antidote should uniformly in morals have a downward tendency.

Amidst the high importance of moral training to the individual, there is also a national and provincial tone of morals contingent on other circumstances, which is not to be measured precisely according to the amount of religious instruction communicated, but according to the *practical* direction which such intellectual teaching or instruction gives to the feelings and affections,—in one word, from the amount of moral training afforded, come from what quarter it may, — parents, schoolmasters, or the higher orders of society, and these influences act and re-act upon the community at large by the *Sympathy of Numbers.* Thus, therefore, there is found in the same kingdom possessing the same amount of religious and secular *instruction*, one town, which may be noted for its high sense of integrity—whilst another is found low and grovelling. One is of sober, and what are called moral habits, and another proverbial for drunkenness and dissipation. One place is renowned for the kindness, hospitality, courteousness, and even generosity of its inhabitants—whilst another in the immediate vicinity is noted for evil speaking, rudeness, and even hard heartedness. Individuals in each locality no doubt are to be found whose conduct is the reverse of the general tone of the place in which they live; but it is wonderful how *sympathy* influences many even of principle, and carries them marvellously along the tide with those with whom they associate.

Our forefathers we believe, had quite as large an amount of religious knowledge as we have. In one point, however, they had not the training. They were not morally trained to give to chariable and religious objects what they might or ought to have given. Neither are we, although in these days persons are to be found who give a pound or a hundred pounds whose pious ancestors would have contented themselves with giving a shilling, or at the most a pound. This process of training, not merely of religious instruction, we believe, but of moral training, will go on until a future generation will make willing sacrifices of which we at present can scarcely dream. Let us proceed, therefore, *early* to train the young to right practical as well as theoretical principles, and glorious results will assuredly follow.* Our

* See Appendix E.

well-trained youth, it is to be hoped, would become christian and kind-hearted men.

On looking around on all existing institutions, private and public, whereby the mass of a people can be morally and intellectually elevated, I see no machinery adapted to the powerful influence of *the Sympathy of Numbers* equal to the moral training school, or which is likely so quickly and so effectually to change the whole tone of public and of private morals.

What we desire, therefore, is simply to apply this felt and known power to popular education, and it is found to be equally applicable and powerful in the intellectual as in the moral department of the Training system.

By using this principle as an instrument in the process of moral training in the gallery and in the play-ground or uncovered school-room, and having such training schools commensurate with the whole population in town and country, we consider it from experience to be practicable, under God's blessing, to improve the whole tone of public as well as private morals within even a single generation. *

* From Mrs. Ellis's new work, " Prevention better than Cure."

" We now come to the consideration of a very important principle, which owes its establishment, as an element in moral training, to the indefatigable efforts of * * * * It is the SYMPATHY OF NUMBERS.

" Home education, excellent as it may be in other respects, is necessarily deficient in this great power; and hence the

Repeated experiments founded upon the imperfect views I then possessed resulted in 1826-7, in the establishment of a model school for the exhibition of the moral training system, and at the same time what is now termed a

difficulty in private families of effecting any radical change in favour of a higher tone of moral feeling. We readily perceive from observation of the world, that wherever the moral standard is low, where justice and truth are disregarded, and where the gratification of an ungoverned passion is an object generally allowed, that the sympathy of numbers has a fearful, though an indirect weight on the wrong side; for few will venture openly, even in a state of things so low as this to advocate what is acknowledged to be evil. But we should remember for our satisfaction, that the principle is one which possesses the same power of throwing weight on the *right* side; and that by laying hold of this, and skilfully directing its use, we may, in time, establish a different tone of feeling throughout communities, or masses of individuals, provided only, they are entirely, and without reserve, subject to the application of the right means.

" It is a mockery of words to speak of our moral condition being improved by *half* measures, still less by *talking* on the subject, as we have talked too long, without understanding our own words. The wants of our country are urgent; they have been neglected until they now cry out upon us from every lane, and street, and rural village, and densely-peopled city. All other branches of improvement have claimed attention, and have made proportionately rapid progress except this. We consequently require a force to be brought to bear on this great point, not only adequate to the pains bestowed upon the intellectual culture of the young, but of such power as actually to redeem the past, and to impel the moral course of the rising generation upwards, and onwards, until the intellectual progress, already attained, shall be overtaken, and even surpassed."

Normal training Seminary for preparing teachers to practise it. It was *then* established, and is still pursued with the full expectation that the universal extension of the system would prove to be a mighty moral lever of society generally, and in particular the much-desired antidote to the exposed condition of the youth especially of large towns and manufacturing villages, independently of the powerful *reflex influence* the system has proved to have on the parents at home.

Delicate as the ground is on which I propose to tread, truth and duty compel me to state a few facts in regard to the principal systems of education in existence in 1820, or which have since sprung up: not, indeed, to condemn or approve of persons or particular societies, but in all humility to analyse principles, and to endeavour to show what is the desideratum.

THE OLD ROTE SYSTEM.

Previous to 1820 I never visited any school upon a better principle than the above-mentioned, nor heard of one. The system was almost entirely one of the repetition or committal of sounds to memory, without explanation; and it was a wonder if a question of any kind was put by the master from any point of the lesson which the children read or repeated, unless indeed the questions and answers were set forth in a book, in the form of a catechism. There was little or no exercise of mind, *no intellectual training*, no natural illustrations given through which the words used might give the idea intended to be communicated to the children. As to moral training it was never thought of nor practised, it being supposed a settled truth that instruction is synonymous with training; that the verbal or intellectual knowledge of scriptural or scientific terms is about the same thing as the reduction of them into ideas and to practical use.

I shall not attempt to illustrate this mode of teaching by any of the innumerable facts that have passed under our notice. There is not space, and they are too ludicrous in many instances almost to obtain credence. They would serve little purpose, save to excite a smile. It is much to be regretted that this *old rote system*, in by far the majority of instances, is still the practice in the schools of the United Kingdom; and the proof is that children generally, who have been taught to read, write, and cast accounts, are not found on trial to understand what they have read; nor do the lessons of scripture appear to have made any impression on their conduct in life. *They have not been trained.* Broken-down soldiers, antiquated dames, uneducated men, and any one whatever he might be, that was unfit for anything else, could and *can* manage *such* a school. And as parents among the working classes consider simple reading, &c., to be the all in all in education, which can be given by any one who can simply read himself, so the accomplished teacher is compelled to reduce his fees to the low standard of others; and cultivated men have no temptation to follow a profession in which they must be half starved.

Now let us remember that while the wealthy classes may have the minds of their children exercised in grammar schools and universities, all the cultivation the poor and working classes receive must be had in the elementary English school. If their minds are not exercised there, they cannot in general educate themselves afterwards; they cannot read intelligently, or add to their stock of knowledge. They have not the means nor the opportunity of doing so.

I may state my experience in 1816, in my own Sabbath school in Glasgow, in regard to the results of the intellectual culture of our much boasted scriptural schools; we shall state the experience of a young gentleman, ten years afterwards, and we shall also state an investigation made in 1845, on a more extended scale, not confined to one locality, and exhibiting a fair sample of the extent of knowledge and moral culture of young persons collected from all parts of the city and suburbs, and employed in four highly respectable factories in which the lowest of the people are not employed.*

* See Appendix B.

SCOTTISH PAROCHIAL SCHOOL SYSTEM.

There is no particular mode of intellectual communication required in the parish schools of Scotland. The master may teach how or in what manner he pleases, and he may employ monitors or not as he thinks fit. He must, however, teach the reading of the Scriptures, and the children must be taught to commit the Westminster Assembly's shorter catechism to memory. It is not necessary that the master should analyse either. The system is unsuited for moral training, having no play-ground, or uncovered school-room attached to the ordinary school-room, for the development of the real dispositions and habits of the pupils at play, which is the real life of the child. Nor is the intellectual department of the covered school-room of that nature, or so systematised, as to enable the master *to spend the requisite time* for superintendence and the revision of their moral conduct which the picturing out system in connection with the gallery affords. When moral training is added, and the picturing out system in connection with the gallery training lessons is adopted, the Scottish system will then present the fulfilment of its great reformer's earnest wish, viz., " the godly *upbringing* of the youth of the land."

We highly approve of the practice in the Scottish parochial schools, of boys and girls being together in the same classes. Much of the moral feeling of the rural population of Scotland has arisen from this practice.

We object to the Scottish parochial school system, because the teacher is burdened with a task he cannot accomplish in a proper manner, viz., the teaching of children of all ages, and in every branch of education from the alphabet to the classics and mathematics. Proper classification, therefore, is out of the question, even with an assistant, who is generally untrained. The master, however, in process of time, may have trained himself to a system of his own more or less efficient.

We have already said, that there is actually no particular system of communication pursued in the parochial schools. Every man has his own system. Up to the year 1820, the old rote system was all but universal. Since that period a few of the most intelligent teachers have introduced many improvements of modern times, and among these some of the peculiarities of the Training system. We admire this part of the arrangement, however, that each school is attached to a particular church, over which the minister, as representative of the Presbytery, has a superintendence and a certain degree of control, and that the heritors of the parish are obliged by law to provide a school-house, dwelling-house, and a salary of from £22 to £34 of annual endowment; in consequence of which the fees charged are so low as to be within the reach of the poorest family of the parish. This we believe is the real cause why the Scottish parochial school system has met with such applause from foreigners, as the mighty moral renovator of our rural society. It has been useful, no doubt, but it has been only subordinate, and forms but *one* part of a great moral machine, which it would be foreign to our purpose at present to analyse.

For reasons already stated it is not a system suited to meet the condition of the population of towns. It does not meet that great overpowering practical principle, THE SYMPATHY OF NUMBERS, and, therefore, if our large towns and manufacturing villages are to be morally and intellectually elevated, what the old parochial system cannot do must be accomplished by some other.

Many of the most intelligent teachers of the parochial schools have expressed a strong desire to add moral training, and to adopt the intellectual mode of the training system, both in Scriptural and in scientific or secular lessons, but the heritors of the parishes have almost uniformly declined being at the expense of providing a playground, or a gallery with suitable apparatus.

THE PRUSSIAN SYSTEM.

This system has been celebrated throughout the world so highly, and is so frequently appealed to as the standard of perfection, that it is almost presumptuous to state that it embodies any one point or feature from which we must dissent. Like the parochial school system of Scotland, it has been pronounced all but perfect. The Prussian system has *no mode* of communication. A long list of books and subjects to be taught and of general rules is its system. Parents are compelled by law under pain of fine or imprisonment, to send their children to school, from the age of seven to fourteen years,* unless they are able to prove that they are giving them a competent education at home, of which the school committee are to be the judges. The state provides for the schoolmaster both during active service and when he is past it. So essential is the point of maintenance deemed, that the words of the Prussian law speaking in the King's name are, " It is our will that in the maintenance of every school this be regarded as the most important object, and take precedence of all others." There is no difficulty, therefore, in complying with the enactment; and during the extended period of seven years, the variety of branches can easily be progressively undertaken. It is widely different in this country where parents must pay the schoolmaster's fee, and where children are seldom permitted to remain at school longer than simply to acquire the merest elements of reading, writing, and arithmetic. From the long period

---

* " Five," says M. Cousin in his Report, " is the age fixed, but seven is that at which education is rigidly enforced."

of instruction the teachers enjoy, first in the primary and middle schools and lastly in the Normal seminaries, of course they may be well educated, but each master is left to exercise his own judgment as to the mode of communication. No one principle is laid down as a rule.

Moral training does not form a part of the system, and were it enjoined it could not be accomplished, as the master is not permitted to give religious instruction from the Bible, which is the only standard of morals, and on which alone all moral training ought to be based. The religious instruction is left to the priest of the particular persuasion to which the parents of the children belong, Roman Catholic or Protestant. According to M. Cousin's report the system is chiefly suited to rural districts, as in the Scottish system. It is not adapted to the condition of the youth of large towns. It does not embrace that most powerful practical principle, THE SYMPATHY OF NUMBERS.

From M. Cousin's report the questioning and explanatory mode is followed, and except the provisions already stated we see no superiority in the Prussian system whatever, over the methods adopted in the schools of our best masters. It is not religious as far as the master is concerned—there is no bible training—no direct moral training. Such a system would not prove an antidote to the demoralising influence of our large towns and manufacturing villages.*

* The following is from the Foreign Quarterly Review for

We do not rest our authority on M. Cousin's report alone, highly trust-worthy as it is. We do so on one more closely connected with ourselves, viz. that of our late worthy Rector, Mr. John M'Crie, son of the author of the lives of Knox and Melville.

In the year 1836, while yet on the Continent, and before he had seen the Training system pursued in the model schools of the Normal se-

November 1844, Review of " Benebre's Theory and Practice of Education in Germany."

The Reviewer observes :—" This is the favorite distinction made by that * * * Mr. ——— in Glasgow. ' To instruct,' says the northern Philanthropist, ' is comparatively an easy matter—a retail dealing in special commodities, a dexterous juggling with so many balls; but in order to educate you must not merely instruct, but you must *train*, to have an educational system at all, it must be a ' training system.'

" This is what the inquisitive traveller will find written in large letters, in the lobby of the Normal Seminary of Glasgow; and to the same purpose, the German tells us that *instruction* deals almost exclusively in mere intellectual notions of external dexterity, while *education* has mainly to do with the formation of the character, through the emotions.

" There is nothing new in this, certainly, but it is a great and important truth : a mere *teacher* does not do half his work, he must work on the heart and on the habits, as well as on the head of his pupils.

" A brain is not the only part of a boy, and his brain is a thing of living growth and arborescence ; not an empty box which an adult can furnish with labelled tickets of various arts and sciences, and then say ' my work is done, behold an educated young gentleman.'"

minary at Glasgow, in actual operation, Mr. M'Crie was chosen Rector; and he was appointed to spend nine months in Germany and France, and closely to examine the Prussian system, as practised in both of these countries. We waited anxiously for his return in February, 1837, that we might alter our system if judged necessary, or at least engraft upon it whatever might be valuable, in this highly celebrated system of education. Mr. M'Crie was an excellent German scholar, and therefore had the best opportunity of examining the schools, and forming a correct judgement. When he entered upon his office and had acquired a knowledge of the Training system, as established in the Glasgow Normal Seminary, he did not change or modify any one of its features, but continued every one of its peculiarities, reporting that all that was valuable in the Prussian system was already embodied in ours, and that in some points we had gone before it. He preferred our mode of Picturing-out in words in the intellectual department, whether in scientific or bible lessons, and as to Moral training, he stated that in Prussia it was never attempted. This was so far satisfactory, considering that the Training system had been established in ignorance of what was going on in Prussia.

The seminary had the misfortune to be deprived of Mr. M'Crie's valuable services by death, nine months after his induction.

THE INFANT SCHOOL SYSTEM.

This system in practice is conducted very variously. Some schools having play-grounds, others without them. Some give lessons from a few of the historical parts of Scripture from picture boards.* Others, again, scarcely touch upon any religious point whatever. The lessons are not read from the Bible itself. Some teachers confine themselves to printed lists of questions and answers on every subject, and they form ellipses by leaving out a single word, or, perhaps, two, which, when filled up by the children, are either so obvious as to form no exercise of mind whatever beyond the verbal memory, or they are mere guesses. Natural history forms an important feature in the daily lessons from objects and picture sheets.

The chief peculiarities of the infant school system lie in the practical proof, that physical exercises, properly applied, tend to produce good order and obedience; and, also, that if you present objects to the attention of very young children, they are perfectly capable of being interested by them, and having their observing faculties cultivated and strengthened. This many mothers have discovered long ago, but the infant

* In general to the number of twenty-four sheets, or from single texts printed on large sheets and hung up on the walls of the schoolroom.

school system first exhibited it as a fact in school education. These points are highly important as parts of any system for training the child, whether in school or in the family.

Infant education, when a play-ground is in use, and when the children are carefully superintended by a master or mistress, is a blessing to a child, for perhaps a single year, but after that period children, generally, lose their relish for the intellectual exercises, from the monotonous repetition of answers from the same lesson-boards, and confined to mere external facts without enlisting the understanding by *picturing out in words* the various relations, associations, analogies, &c. of every subject presented, and becoming more and more minute as the children advance in knowledge of external things. The few and meagre Bible lessons also, which are repeated to weariness, fail in forming even a basis for moral training. The infant system may be considered, therefore, a complete, or stereotyped, one, for a limited period of the child's life, and cannot be made initiatory to his subsequent education.

Infant schools in general have proved a failure; not that they are not for a time extremely *interesting* to look at, or that so far they do not make a favourable impression upon the children, but they have failed in producing those permanent, intellectual, or moral results so fondly anticipated, because the system is too much one of teaching, and too little of training; and, also, because it has been thought that any sort of person may

conduct the system, consequently, the least cultivated men and women have generally been placed
in the infant school.

This is a grievous mistake, for the cultivation
of infants under six years of age is by far the most
important and influential of all departments in
education.

Infant *teaching* is the most easy thing imagin-
able. Infant *training* the most difficult. Almost
any sort of person may become an infant *teacher*,
—the highest powers are required and may be
exerted in infant *training*. It is not necessary,
indeed, that the master should be either a classical
or mathematical scholar, but he will fail unless
his powers are of that class and description that
might render him successful in both. In fact, he
must be an intelligent, well-educated, shrewd,
sensible, cultivated, pious man. To be able to
communicate to infants the *outlines* of every subject secular and sacred—to train the young unso-
phisticated, impressible mind and moral habits,
in language and manners simple enough, requires
the highest powers.

The trainer himself, therefore, must possess ten
times the amount of knowledge he *apparently* is
called upon to express. Infant *teaching* schools
have failed—infant *training* schools, conducted
on natural and scriptural principles, have never
failed. To teach facts may be an easy matter—
to train the youthful ignorant mind, to give reasons and draw lessons, and to mould the moral
character intelligently and practically is certainly
not so easy.

I consider the infant department the highest point of attainment in the training of a normal student, whether he intends to become a trainer in the juvenile or more advanced departments. If he succeeds in this with young children, he never fails in training the older ones in any branch, mentally or morally.

The training system, as established in the model schools of the Free Normal Seminary at Glasgow is conducted on the principles now recommended, the infant school being termed *initiatory* to the other four departments for older children. In it, therefore, the pupil-trainer commences his practical studies how to train "the whole man." Here he is, as it were, first *pulverised*, and having finished his course of training, in what has been termed the advanced departments, and thus, having been moulded, he is placed again in the initiatory department to receive his highest polish. Some of our best juvenile masters were trained in the seminary when we had only one initiatory school for infants. Without an initiatory school having infants under six years of age, I consider a normal training seminary must be defective. The intelligent and practical reader will acknowledge that simplicity is the highest attainment of a teacher or trainer of youth.

The Home and Colonial Society for training teachers still bears the name of the Infant School System. The truly benevolent superintendents of this institution of late years have made many additions to the system, and we believe have considerably altered and improved the mode of communication, so that it can scarcely now be classed under the title Infant School System. We should, however, still desire to see the natural simplicity of " picturing out in words," thoroughly followed in the intellectual department both in the secular and Bible gallery lessons. A desire for the best interests of pupils and students powerfully stimulates all who are in the direction of this institution.

BOROUGH ROAD, OR BRITISH AND FOREIGN SCHOOL SYSTEM.

Whilst the old rote system is an undefined random or *stuffing* system, and the Scottish Parochial is peculiar, chiefly for its connexion with the Church, the free use of the Bible and its partial endowments, the Borough Road is well defined, both in the arrangements of school apparatus, the mode of communication by monitors, its non-connection with any particular church—its rare use of the Bible, except by the master, and the careful avoidance of any explanation whatever that might bias the minds of the pupils to any peculiar understanding of the words read, and the circumstance, also, that those adopting its principles are sent out, as the title bears, to British and foreign parts, only after being trained in the establishment in the Borough Road.

We have often admired the pains taken to devise this plan, and to render it approvable to all parties, and to make it one of thorough intellectual education,—the ardour, also, by which the whole has been prosecuted by its worthy secretary and its no less devoted head master; but, however painful, we must dissent from some of its leading principles.

First, I do not think it possible to have a perfect system of education conducted by monitors; nay, the reports of the Government inspectors prove it to be an entire failure. Masters may be *tame* and imperfect enough under any system, but monitors *must* be so. They are, at best, but apprentices in the art. They may teach facts, but they cannot *train*. Much injury oftentimes arises to themselves from the elevation over their fellows, which is visible by the self-important manner and strut of their official dignity. A perfect system cannot be accomplished by monitors, unless their services be confined to mere servile, or matter of fact work, in which case they may profitably assist the master, and occupy the time and attention of the children.

We cannot approve of boys and girls being in separate schools at the early age of six to twelve years. This is common in all the schools of England for all ranks, and not peculiar to the Borough Road system. Still, we think that if a proper conduct between boys and girls be a part of moral training, (and we are sure that the conductors of this institution earnestly desire the moral improvement of their pupils), then boys and girls may be told or taught what to do, but they cannot be *trained* to act properly towards each other if kept in separate apartments. The very evils desired to be avoided are, in a measure, generated by the separative principle.

We object to the fact of the Bible not being uniformly put into the hands of the children, and, also, because, while a portion may be read by the master in the hearing of the children each day, he must not analyse, or catechise, or explain. We believe no catechism is in use, and it is unnecessary, since no explanation is permitted. We are stating objections to the principle, not to the many excellent men who conduct it. But if young men, as students in the institution, are trained from day to day to avoid exercising their own or their pupils' minds on the truths of Scripture, may it not be—is it not likely that their love for the Word of God may be weakened, and that, on being placed in a school of their own, Bible instruction, or rather Bible reading, may not become the merest form, and that religion will virtually be excluded from the entire system? Most certainly, if not explained, Scriptural truth cannot be made the basis of moral training, even if adopted in this far-famed and magnificent institution. Play-grounds not being a part of the system, there cannot be direct moral training; because there is not development of character and dispositions.

Thirty years practical experience with children, and twenty years with 1,200 grown students of all denominations, have proved to me that the full analysis and picturing out of Scripture in its emblems, precepts, promises, threatenings, and general history, is not only safe, but meets with the most cordial sympathy of persons of all denominations, and proves itself to be *one of the highest intellectual exercises which can be engaged in.* A vast deal more of science is necessary to elucidate its emblems than at first sight appears. The non-explanation principle was determined on, we believe, from the purest motives for peace and unity. But the truth of God surely cannot suffer from the honest exposition of it, and with children and students of all religious denominations, for above twenty years, our masters have found no difficulty. All has been the most perfect unity, and, if not told, one could scarcely have guessed to what communion any one belonged.

This department of the training system of education, as we have already stated, is termed

" BIBLE TRAINING,"

and which, with praise and prayer, occupies the first hour's exercise of each morning.

For aught I know, many most Christian men who have been trained in the Borough Road school may break through these rules and explain the Scriptures to their pupils and place Bibles in the hands of all of them. I should expect, however, that they would rather follow the model according to which they had been trained, and a visitor, however highly pleased with the plan which he observes going on, would naturally say, " You are not teaching according to the British and Foreign School Society's system."

This system presents so many attractive and valuable points in education that we have been enchanted with the interesting sight of the various departments. Nothing but a regard for the interests of the rising generation could compel us to say that the Borough Road system is not the one, as a whole, that we would establish as the moral renovator of the youth of our country,— most certainly not of large towns.

NATIONAL SCHOOL SYSTEM OF ENGLAND.

All that we have taken the liberty of stating in regard to monitors, and the separation of the sexes,* under the head " Borough Road system," is equally applicable to the National Society, and need not be repeated. Much more might be said on both subjects, but we forbear.

The *Old Rote System* is more generally followed than in the British and Foreign system. The teaching of the latter, although by no means sufficiently natural or simple, is yet decidedly more intellectual; but of late many individual clergymen,† in various districts of England, have introduced, and are rapidly introducing, the highest improvements which modern times have suggest-

* Every clergyman and director knows the difficulties of providing and retaining female teachers for the girls' school.
† See Appendix D.

ed ; and although moral training, as a direct
exercise, does not exist in the schools under
the National School system, a play ground and
gallery and picturing out in words forming no
part of the system ; yet, *they may be* introduced
consistently with its principles, and the Scriptures
may be read *and fully explained* by the master.
This, however, is seldom attempted. In general
the process is all *teaching*, no *training*. The understanding of the pupils is seldom exercised. The
system in practice makes a very slight impression
indeed on the moral or intellectual *habits* of the
pupils.

We object to confining the analysis of Scripture so generally to short extracts of the historical
parts of Scripture and the Church Catechism,
without picturing out or causing the children to
draw the natural lesson which each picture, as
it is represented, affords. The catechism, or
course, is taught, but it should be analysed, and its
doctrines proved from Scripture, and it would be
preferable to read the history of Scripture characters *from the Book itself*, as bringing with it more
directly the authority of its great Author.

The Bible, with explanation, being perfectly
permissible in the National Schools, whatever the
practice may be, — moral training, based on
Scripture, may, therefore, be the more easily introduced into the schools of the National Society
than into those of the Borough Road. It will be
admitted that there cannot be moral training
without a moral standard. The only unchangea-

ble standard is the Bible, and to be efficient, its plain meaning and import must be understood. The shell of *true* education or *training* may be introduced into the National Schools, no barrier being set against the explanation of Scripture by the master, provided only that each school were furnished with a gallery, and each school-room have a play-ground or uncovered school-room attached ; and, also, the substance were *the masters trained how to superintend the children at play, and afterwards to review their conduct and to picture out the various lessons in the gallery, whether scriptural, scientific, or elementary.* The idea, so practically followed out, must be given up that the mere reading of the Scriptures and committal of the catechism and tasks to memory, will suffice morally or intellectually to elevate mankind. As well as the practice, there must be a thorough analysis and understanding of the subject of the lesson. Truth never can lose by being fully pictured out. Thus, the trainer may render the school a fruitful nursery for the Church.

THE IRISH SYSTEM OF EDUCATION.

We are aware that in the establishment of this system difficulties presented themselves which scarcely required to be noticed in England.— Still, however, we ought to consider how far the benevolent object is gained by its establishment, —an object, which has in view the *education* and elevation of the minds of the Irish population.

We shall just touch upon one or two points, the result of our personal observations. In company with a friend, I visited the south of Ireland in 1837, and looked into every school in town and country upon which I could set my eyes. I found no questions put, no explanations of any lessons given, secular or sacred, no exercise of thought whatever. The whole was one continued reading or repetition of sounds, without attaching any meaning; the movements of the pen on paper or on slate taking place from morning till evening. It appeared to me that the memory of words and figures alone formed the ultimatum of the education afforded. It was better certainly in the Model School at Dublin; but at the time of my visit there was not one student in the institution under training. Teachers of some of the country schools confessed to me, that although they were not permitted to explain Scripture during school hours, yet, as the clock struck three, without the children moving from their seats, they taught the children the dogmas of the Church of Rome from their own catechism. *During school hours,* in one place I heard the children taught by the teacher, while reading the miracle of Peter's walking on the water to meet Jesus, that Peter was the first Pope. This was done by the teacher to show me that children might be catechised in a Catholic school. This school was endowed with £17 10s. annually from the Government grant.

I am fully satisfied that the brilliant Irish mind can never be intellectually elevated by this system—that, morally, it can scarcely have any improving effect whatever. It only exercises the eye, the fingers, and the verbal memory, and therefore has been, and must continue to prove a failure.

THE INTELLECTUAL SYSTEM.

In speaking of the intellectual system which has been introduced into many schools since the year 1830, we understand it to be a thorough verbal explanation and catechising of the scholars on the part of the teachers. The system may be applied to a greater or less extent to any other. It has been introduced by teachers of well-informed minds, and, generally speaking, of some claim to genius.

This intellectual mode of questioning and verbal explanation may be applied to Scripture, to science, and to any literary subject. In Scripture, practically, it is generally confined to historical facts. In other branches it presents a thorough verbal criticism. Etymology — the meaning of words, and mental arithmetic, present its most important features.

We consider the intellectual system, highly as it has improved the method of communication, as not simple enough in the language required to be used, and not natural enough—familiar illustrations and analogy not forming requisite parts of the system.

There is too much teaching or telling, and too little training; too great a stimulus is required for the minds of those whose sensibilities are tender, although they may be thoroughly acute and comprehensive.

The system requires the important additions of analogy and familiar illustrations, couched in language suited to the capacity of all the pupils. We are not aware of moral training forming a component part of the plan of any school taught on this system.

All that is valuable in the Intellectual system is included in the simple and more natural mode of the Training system, without the high stimulus of prizes and places, without retarding the progress of the intellectually strong, or of frightening so as to retard the less highly gifted, or of running the risk of weakening the moral sense of any of the pupils. Under the training system such high stimulants are rejected as sometimes injurious and always unnecessary.

It is almost unnecessary to state here, that the highest intellectual training, we conceive, from all past experience, is not sufficient of itself to morally, or even intellectually, elevate our youthful population. There is a sympathy between the exercise of the moral and intellectual faculties and habits that greatly elevates the latter, so that the moral cannot be exercised without at the same time strengthening and elevating the intellectual.

Of late years we hear of —
>The Simultaneous System,
>The Gallery System,
>The Elliptical System,
>The Glasgow System,
>The Suggestive System, and
>The Normal System.

But as all these have been more or less copied and introduced into popular schools from the Training System, which was established at Glasgow, it is unnecessary to allude to them in particular.

NORMAL SEMINARIES FOR PREPARING TEACHERS AND TRAINERS.

Twenty-four years ago, when I first proposed to train teachers to the system which I fondly hoped might, by God's blessing, elevate the mass of our sunken population in large towns, in other words, by moral training, in addition to religious and secular instruction, the idea of such a prerequisite scarcely existed in the public mind. Now, however, the necessity is becoming pretty universally felt that schoolmasters ought to be previously trained as in every other art. Something has been done—a first step has been made. It is only, however, a first step. We have a few training seminaries as a commencement, but they are not all on the right system. Some of these are purely intellectual, others scarcely so. Very few train, or even profess to train the entire "child" morally, religiously, intellectually, and physically. Not only would we desire to see all conducted on the true system of training the "whole man," but that the number should be increased at least tenfold. At first we imagined that three months would suffice to train a well-educated man, but now we are quite satisfied that neither six nor twelve months are sufficient for the purpose, and if our future school trainers, even after passing through the common normal school, are to be instructed in the higher branches of knowledge, which they are to communicate, as well as the arts of communication and moral training, then the period of attendance in our normal seminaries must be greatly extended, and of course greater sacrifices of money on the part of the Government and the public will be required.

In taking a comparative view of the several bearings of the normal seminaries—diocesan and other training schools for training teachers, we would not determine the comparative value of any one from a single case or two either of great success or of failure. We would take the general tendency naturally deducible from each system, and the general effect upon the minds and manners of the children as exhibited by the mass of the students who, on leaving the seminaries, have been permitted to practise their art.

From a careful survey of all the systems of education which existed in 1820, or which have since sprung up, it appears that not any one presents the aspect of *direct moral training. The sympathy of numbers*, which is particularly strong and influential in youth, has not been rendered sufficiently available. The intellectual department in some, although greatly improved, is yet too verbal, and by no means so natural and simple as it might be. Natural and familiar illustrations, always interesting to the young, are seldom given, and these not systematically. Physical health has been sadly neglected, and no provision made for its promotion by a play-ground, or uncovered school-room. In fact, although moral training was desired to be introduced, the idea is impracticable, as the master, under the present modes, has not the requisite time for superintendence at play, and the intellectual and moral review of the children's conduct afterwards.

When the school premises are properly arranged, *and the master trained to conduct the system,* it works in beauteous harmony and efficiency, and its power and simplicity startles all but those practically engaged in it. As already stated, in the absence of a more simple, natural, and Scriptural system, we must present THE TRAINING SYSTEM as the mighty desideratum for the moral, religious, physical, and intellectual elevation of the youth of our country, but *more particularly of large towns and manufacturing villages.* That it would be so we firmly believed from its commencement; that it is so has been established by the concurrent testimony of many thousand clergymen, directors of schools, poor-law commissioners, noblemen, and the parents of the children thus educated. From the latter we hold 700 written testimonials, more laudatory in many instances, we believe, than would be admitted by many of our grave educationalists; its success, therefore, is a matter of fact and of history.

The system now recommended, if commenced at the early age of three years (for the training system is fitted for the earliest as well as the latest period of a child's education), would enable children to be well instructed and trained intellectually and morally by the time when they may be legally employed in public factories. A thorough training course of ten years would thus be secured, and would render unnecessary any Factory Education Bill, as the boy or girl of thirteen years of age would afterwards be able to carry on their education themselves in the evenings, and they would understand what they read; and from the habit of mind and moral culture acquired in the training school it is hoped they would also be able to compare and distinguish truth from error. " Prevention is indeed better than cure." It is too late then to cure ignorance, when the opportunity has been lost of acquiring knowledge, or to form good habits when evil ones are already firmly established.

What are the details of that system which embraces the cultivation of the whole human being, and of which a treatise of 500 pages* presents little more than an outline, we cannot presume

* The Training System, seventh edit. Blackie and Son, Warwick-square.

to unfold within the compass of a short pamphlet. Suffice it to say, it is simple and powerful, as is the steam-engine, and may be rendered as influential in the moral world as the latter is in the commercial.

The system is perfectly elastic, and suited to the natural capacity of all. All men are not alike gifted by nature; all men were not intended to be school trainers any more than portrait painters. Each schoolmaster is free to exercise his natural powers, and may exercise those of his pupils according to their capabilities, whether argumentative, illustrative, imaginative, or matter of fact.

This, termed the Training System from the scriptural command, "Train up," &c. was the first, we believe, to present a method of education, by which the child might be trained from infancy to manhood, without any change of system morally and intellectually, and in all branches.

It so happens also that the normal seminary at Glasgow was the first institution in Great Britain in which teachers were trained to their art. The institution commenced with only one school-house, and other premises, play-ground, gallery, &c., for the youngest children. It has been removed three times to more extended premises, as the departments for older children were added; and a fourth time it has been transferred with the same trainers and the same superintendence, to premises provided by the Education Committee of the Free Church of Scotland. Teachers of all communions and of both sexes are regularly under training—Episcopalian, Wesleyan, Presbyterian, Independent, &c. All act in harmony under the same religious, intellectual, and moral training; and having spent a sufficient time in the institution to acquire a practical knowledge of the system, all embark in the prosecution of it with enthusiasm.

The necessity of establishing moral training was apparent. The question was, how then could it be added to the ordinary school branches where masters and scholars on the old system were already fully occupied? The gallery and the *simultaneous* principle of picturing out in words* were found to save the requisite time; and there is now presented not merely moral training as a new principle in popular education, but also a new and more natural mode of cultivating the intellectual powers in every department. These two points, moral training and picturing out in words, form the chief peculiarities of the training system.

* During the debate on Lord Ashley's Factory Bill, in 1842, and in speaking of the Education grant proposed for that year, the Right Hon. Sir J. Graham, amidst other friendly expressions, and particularly of this part of the training system, said, "I consider it to be the greatest discovery in education of modern times." On another occasion, during a private interview, eight years ago, with a noble lord high in her Majesty's councils, his lordship thus expressed himself: "I perceive that all the improvements in education worthy of notice, which have lately been introduced into the schools of England, may be traced to the establishment of the Glasgow Normal Seminary."

We shall simply state a few facts as to the extension and progress of the system.

1.—The students trained during the first few years of the institution were appointed to schools in Scotland, a few to England, and a considerable number to the colonies. Of these, one-third may be stated as for juvenile and two-thirds for infant schools.

2.—Immediately after a visit to the seminary of J. P. Kay Shuttleworth, and C. Tuffnel, Esqrs., in 1837, and before the model schools, &c., were concentrated into one building, the Poor-law Commissioners of various counties in England, induced by the kind statements of these gentlemen, ordered a large number as trainers of the neglected children of the poor-law unions in England; and, with an enlightened policy, continue doing so till the present day. The result of this experiment has been highly satisfactory and striking, both in an intellectual and moral point of view, and high testimonials in favour of the system and the trainers have been granted by the neighbouring clergy, by chaplains of the unions, and the guardians. There has, however, been this alloy; that, from the oftentimes severe and even degrading labour to which the guardians of some unions exposed the schoolmasters, they were naturally disposed to leave on the first opportunity presented of a more comfortable and suitable situation. The success of the training system in the unions, naturally led many of the clergy, who were desirous of improving the style of education in their own parishes, to accept of their services, and the consequence has been, that full three-fourths of the whole number appointed to the unions, have been induced to leave. While many of the boards of guardians have thrown obstacles in the way of the school-trainer's permanency of office, other unions have acted with the utmost kindness and liberality. The Poor-law Commissioners were certainly the first to extend the system in their own department, throughout England. To Mr. Shuttleworth, secretary to the committe of Council, as the great educationalist of the day, a deep debt of gratitude, is due for his untiring perseverance in this cause. Mr. Shuttleworth introduced six or seven trainers into Norwood, and several into Battersea college, and recommended others for the colonies, two of whom were appointed as rectors for normal training seminaries in Colombo and Kandy, island of Ceylon.

3.—From clergymen of the Church of England, during the last eight or ten years, there has been a large demand for trainers; some for infant schools, but more generally for juvenile national schools; and we may state, that very generally they have been at the expense of adding play-grounds and erecting galleries for the prosecution of the system, or if new buildings were to be erected, the whole premises were arranged according to our plan. I may also state, that as we have only a very limited supply of Episcopalian students under training in the seminary at any one time, and the demand being five or six times greater than our ability to supply, these clergymen have generally accepted of Presbyterian students, whenever they were disposed to conform to the English service,—which was generally done. Many clergymen and directors not connected with the unions, have ordered trainers from time to time. From a number of congregational ministers and directors in England and Wales, we have also received orders, and to whom we have sent trainers. The number to Ireland has been very limited not exceeding twenty in all.

4.—By order and permission of the Right Honourable the Home Secretary, about three or four years ago, two trainers were appointed to take charge of the lads in the upper prison of Parkhurst, Isle of Wight. This reformatory prison contains about 200 young men and boys, under sentencè of transportation. This almost national experiment of the introduction of the training system into prisons, under christian and well-trained masters, has produced moral results which were scarcely to be anticipated. So thorough a change has taken place on a large number of the young men, that at the request of the Right Honourable the Home Secretary, and with the approbation of the benevolent governor of the prison, the chaplain and school-trainers, Her most gracious Majesty, during the present year, has been pleased to grant a free pardon to a large number. About forty have proceeded to Port-Philip; and twenty one, by the kind interposition of friends, have found suitable masters in England and Scotland, and I understand are doing well —in many cases displaying the most decidedly pious and christian conduct. I subjoin a short notice, which appeared in one of our public journals. The whole matter reflects high honour on the government and all concerned.*

5.—Several Wesleyan students having been trained in the institution at Glasgow, and their success in England being apparent, after a careful inspection of the parent institution by some of their number, the Wesleyan Educational Committee resolved, that both at home and abroad, they would adopt " the moral training system " in all their schools. With this view they selected the most pious well-educated young men and women they could find throughout their congregations, and sent them to Glasgow for six or nine months to be trained, supporting them at the same time out of their public funds. During 1843—4, difficulties arose in regard to supporting the institution at Glasgow, from the unsettled state of church matters, and the seminary being dependent upon, and supported only, by private individuals, there was an accumulated debt of nearly £12,000. At this juncture in order that the system might be maintained in efficiency and the training of teachers continued, the Wesleyan Committee most handsomely agreed to grant £600 for one year, provided we trained for them sixty students, and this in addition to supporting their students during the ordinary course

* See Appendix E.

of training. The usual fee charged for each student, in ordinary cases, is simply £3 3s., which the Wesleyan Committee has continued to pay for all which have been sent since. During the last few years the number trained belonging to this denomination is 265, nearly all of whom are actively employed as trainers throughout England.

The Wesleyan Conference, two years ago, having determined on establishing a Normal training seminary or college of their own, adopted the most judicious plan of securing immediate and ultimate success in the training of students, by selecting four of the most highly educated persons of their own communion, who had formerly been trained six months, and returned them to Glasgow to undergo twelve or eighteen months additional training. This being accomplished, independently of having a large number of trainers placed in various situations throughout England, from which they may select assistants; they have, at least, four well-trained persons, one of whom may be rector, and three head masters for two departments to commence with, in their projected normal seminary or college. Their official inspector, also, during the last eight years, for the sake of practical information, has repeatedly spent a few weeks in the model schools and students' classes of the institution at Glasgow.

The rector and masters of the parent institution at Glasgow, having had from about ten to twenty years practical experience of the training system,

I would take the liberty of strongly recommending, that all who purpose establishing institutions of this nature, should follow the example now mentioned. Any intelligent well-educated man, indeed, in time, may work himself into the system by persevering patience. But what by himself, or by observing a model training school in operation, would take him seven years to accomplish, may be done under half a dozen experienced trainers in a normal seminary, in as many months.

As it is impossible for the Institution at Glasgow to train as many students as they are likely to require, it is proposed by the Wesleyan body during the present season to erect buildings, and establish a normal training seminary in London under their own immediate management and inspection ; and for this purpose they have purchased one-and-a-half acres of ground, and have procured funds to the amount of £21,000.

The whole of the master-trainers belonging to the parent institution being members of the Free Church of Scotland, the Educational Committee undertook to make the seminary its own, and purchased ground and erected suitable buildings at a cost of about £10,000, which now accommodate the whole Institution—thus preventing the system and the training of students from being at all interrupted.

The number of students in attendance each session during the last three years has been about seventy-five,* and of children in the model schools

* It is surprising, perhaps, that the normal students should have come from so many different quarters. In 1845 they

of the seminary about eight hundred, including one hundred girls in the industrial model school.

This department is for girls above ten years of age, in which sewing, knitting, darning, and finer needle-work are taught, and in which they are also carried forward in other elementary branches in which they may be deficient, such as writing, arithmetic, geography, elements of science, and the arts in regard to household economy and daily bible and moral training. A large proportion of the girls in the seminary, however, remain in the other model schools along with the boys after this age, according to the wish of their parents. We desire not to separate the boys and girls too soon from the ordinary classes, in order that both sexes may benefit by this department in moral as well as intellectual training.

Of these 800 there are children of parents belonging to every variety of religious denomination, Presbyterian, Episcopalian, Wesleyan, Congregational, Baptist, Socinian, Society of Friends, and Roman Catholic. The standard of Bible training is according to the Westminster Assembly's shorter catechism. Party is unknown and unfelt, the sole object being to give the children a substantial, elementary, and scientific educa-

were from fifteen counties of England and eleven of Scotland, and three of Ireland, in all 29 counties. In 1846, from thirty-two counties; and in 1847, from thirty-four counties. Besides four from the West Indies; one from Caffraria; two from Madeira; one from Bombay; and one the schoolmaster of the infantry barracks.

tion, and to instruct them in the plain and simple truths of Scripture, and to train them to practise the virtues and graces set forth in the Divine record. This is one important proof of above twenty years standing, *that it is practicable* for all parties to unite in national education. The secret being, that we never pry into the religious opinions of parents who present their children. So great is the demand for admittance into the model training schools of the normal seminary that now there are generally 100 or 150 names put down, waiting for admittance for weeks previous to the quarter's enrolment. Although, to induce attendance some years ago, we felt it necessary to admit them nearly free of charge.

We admire the benevolent exertions which are now making in regard to the establishment of Ragged and Industrial Schools, for boys of the most abandoned description; but as these are only for a small portion of the population, and not intended to be permanent, and as all such abandoned characters must quickly disappear, were " the Training System" universally established, (which is intended to be a permanent moral and intellectual machine, and has been proved to be suitable for the youth of all classes of society,) we therefore in our normal seminary have not establised model schools termed Ragged or Industrial. As temporary and most valuable expedients, however, for the benefit of the dregs of society in towns we most heartily wish them God speed.'

I trust we have said enough to prove that *teaching is not training*—that the education of the "child" consists not merely in instructing or teaching his head—that intellectual training is not necessarily moral, although moral training cannot be conducted without its being at the same time intellectual—that the cultivation of the "whole man" or "the child" must include the exercise of the affections as well as the physical habits—that the understanding must be cultivated, and the whole based on the unalterable will and law of God as contained in the Scriptures of truth.

I trust also that we have shown that the training of the child cannot be conducted within the walls of an ordinary school-room—that our educational institutions generally are not arranged so as to admit of direct moral training—that facts prove that they are decidedly deficient in moral results—that the systems or modes of communication pursued are scarcely even intellectual —that, in fact, we have been sowing hay seed and expecting to reap corn, and that the fact of teachers not having been trained to their art, but left to make out one of their own more or less efficient, and to cut and carve upon their pupils just as they pleased, has proved one fruitful source of failure. In fine, that until our future teachers and trainers of youth undergo a previous course of training according to some " Norma" or rule under experienced masters, popular education must continue, as it has hitherto been, too much a mere name, and the working classes sink below the level of sober, honest, upright, intelligent and sound-hearted Christians. I venture, therefore, to present the training system, or the moral training school, which was first established at Glasgow, as at least one powerful instrument which for twenty years has been confessedly efficient, and which in the hands of a Christian Church, and fed and nourished by the kind assistance of an enlightened and paternal government, so as to render it available to our whole youthful population, I doubt not, under the Divine blessing, even within a single generation would produce results more cheering and glorious than have ever been exhibited since our first parents were driven out of paradise.

APPENDIX.

A.

From " Moral Training, Infant and Juvenile, as applicable to the condition of the population of large towns," 1834.

" What ought to be done for England and for Ireland and for Scotland ?   We shall commence with the latter, with its population of 2,365,807 (in 1831), for the amount requisite for the two former, with inhabitants nine times in number will, no doubt, to many appear frightful.   But why should we startle at a sum of any extent, when the nation could and did freely vote twenty millions sterling for the noble object of slave emancipation ?   Why not vote one-half of the amount for the extinction of slavery at home—the slavery of mind and of morals ?   Such would be a nobler achievement than Waterloo   itself,   which   cost   the   country   forty   millions sterling.

" What is national wealth without national intelligence, piety, and virtue ?   The former may rapidly increase, yea, even tenfold ; but, destitute of the latter, it will only accelerate our ruin.

" We live in a new and eventful state of things.   Towns are the great sources of wealth, the centres of political power, and the seats of vice and profligacy.   The question is, how can this wealth and political power be properly directed ? how can crime and ignorance be diminished? If this is to be accomplished at all, whatever others may be necessary, we are fully satisfied that the *primary* antidotes to these evils, are schools for infant and juvenile training, and in such numbers as to embrace the whole community.

" By Dr. Clelland's statistical tables for 1831 it appears that the number of infants between the ages of two and six years is about one in eight of the whole population. . . .
*　*　*　*　*　*　*　*　*　*
.　. . . . but as, from several causes, the whole infant population could not be got to attend school at any one time, or might be provided for privately, we have made the calculation for one-sixteenth instead of one-eighth of the population. . . . . . . Each parish of 2,400, therefore, will easily furnish a school of 150 infants under six years of age. . . . . . . The same number of inhabitants will yield twice the number of juveniles between the ages of six and fourteen years, or two schools of 150 each—each school having two masters, ... by deducting one-fourth for the richer classes, or for private schools.

" As the training school and play-ground of the juveniles ought to be, at least, as large as those for the infants, and the proportion in towns being one infant to two juvenile schools, the following will be the results :—
*　*　*　*　*　*　*　*　*　*
" Proper masters, under any system, but more especially in the one under consideration, are the very life and essence of the school. No school ought to have as a superintendent one who has not been properly trained. Hence, the absolute necessity of establishing normal schools for training teachers. . . . . . . Ten normal, (including model) schools, for training teachers would be required for Scotland alone, viz., one in Edinburgh, Glasgow, Aberdeen, Dundee, Perth, Dumfries, St. Andrews, Inverness, Kirkwall and Ayr.

" Ground in Edinburgh and Glasgow is extravagantly high in price; and in some parts of those and other densely built cities, where the moral superintendence of the play-ground is most needed, and sites most difficult to be had, some backhouses would require to be purchased, and pulled down for this purpose. Although, therefore, we must expect such play-grounds to be extremely costly (much higher than our tables show), yet they will be ultimately more economical than jails and bridewells and houses of refuge; besides the change, in whatever quarter, will have a satisfactory influence upon the health as well as the morals of the neighbourhood. We also observe, that although it may be possible, in one or more of the towns, to procure single sites for school-houses, and play-grounds large enough and airy enough, even for less than the lowest sum specified—yet, we believe there is not one of the towns enumerated, where the ground, upon the whole, will not cost considerably more on the average, provided the schools be properly placed—we mean, where they are mostly wanted, in the centre of the population."

TABLES for four of the most populous towns in Scotland, the wants of which, no doubt, equally apply to England.

The number of juvenile schools required being double of those for infants, and they requiring, at least, an equal extent of play-ground, the cost will be as follows :—

SCHOOL-SITES AND PLAY-GROUNDS FOR INFANT TRAINING.

Population of Edinburgh (in 1831) 162,156.   67 School sites.

Supposed cost of School sites, including play-grounds, viz., 100 by 60 feet,	10 at £100 each	£1,000
	20 ,, 200 ,,	4,000
	15 ,, 400 ,,	6,000
	11 ,, 600 ,,	6,600
	11 ,, 1000 ,,	11,000
	67	£28,600

Population of Glasgow (in 1831) 202,426.   84 School sites, 150 scholars each.

Cost of School sites, including play-grounds,	10 at £100 each	£1,000
	25 ,, 200 ,,	5,000
	20 ,, 400 ,,	8,000
	14 ,, 600 ,,	8,400
	15 ,, 1000 ,,	15,000
	84	£37,400

SCHOOL-SITES AND PLAY-GROUNDS FOR JUVENILES.

No. of Schools.	Cost.
134	£57,200
168	74,800

SCHOOL-SITES AND PLAY-GROUNDS FOR INFANT TRAINING.	SCHOOL SITES AND PLAY-GROUNDS FOR JUVENILES.	
	No. of Schools.	Cost.

Population of Aberdeen (in 1831) 58,019. 24 School sites, 150 scholars each.

Cost of School sites and play grounds,

8 at £80 each	£640
10 ,, 200 ,, ...	2,000
6 ,, 300 ,, ...	1,800
——	——
24	£4,440

No. of Schools.	Cost.
48	8,880

Population of Paisley (in 1831) 57,466. 24 School sites, 150 scholars each.

Cost of School sites and play grounds,

15 at £80 each	£1,200
6 ,, 200 ,, ...	1,200
3 ,, 300 ,, ...	900
——	——
24	£3,300

No. of Schools.	Cost.
48	6,600

	No. of Schools.	Cost.
Total number of Schools and their cost	190 £73,740	398 £147,480

Endowments of £50 a year each in addition to School fees:—

199 Masters for infant training, £50 each . . . . £9,950 annually
398 ,, juvenile ditto 50 ,, ... 19,900 ,,

Cost of buildings for training schools, suppose at £350 each erection, say 199 schools for Infants, £69,650
Ditto ditto 398 ditto for Juvenile 139,300

F

SUMMARY.

Brought forward—

Play-grounds and school sites—Infant			£73,740
Ditto	ditto	Juvenile	147,480
Cost of buildings . . . . Infant			69,650
Ditto ditto . . . . . Juvenile			169,300

Cost of establishing juvenile and initiatory
(or infant) schools for the poor and working classes in Edinburgh, Glasgow, Aber- } £430,170
deen, and Paisley, including a partial endowment for the masters for *one year*.

" Of course the whole of this amount would not be required
the first year ; at the same time, if, for such important good,
why lose a moment in its completion? It is a sacrifice
the country can easily bear, and would soon be returned
manifold, in actual comfort, in the saving of poor-rates,
building of jails and penitentiaries, nay, in national security.
It may be proper here to say that the training system, with
its moral superintendence at school, is equally necessary in
such towns as Sheffield, Birmingham, Newcastle, Liverpool,
Leeds, Manchester, Coventry, Dublin, Belfast, and the great
emporium, LONDON, which is at once the most religious,
most enlightened, the wealthiest, and, in too large a proportion of its inhabitants, most ignorant and depraved. Here
the poor are actually smothered with charities ; and yet,
more, perhaps, than any other city, does it stand in need of
an enlightened, systematic parochial influence.

* * * * * * * * * *

. . . . . As at present there is not much above one-
half at school which ought to be in attendance, which may
be seen by reference to reports received from every part of
the kingdom, (taking the Prussian proportion of one-sixth,
which ought to be at school, independent of infants,) the
erection of the schools now proposed, infant and juvenile,
would scarcely displace one respectable private teacher.

" Had the requisite number of schools been very small,
we should have said,—' *Let Government provide the endowments, and the cost of play-grounds, and let the school-houses
be built, wholly or half, by private subscription.*' But the

remedy required is too immediate, we cannot wait with safety on the operation of such a distant and slow process. If we continue to sleep on as heretofore, without putting forth *a thorough* training system of education, there is an under-current of profligacy and vice in all the large towns of the United Kingdom, which, ere long, may overturn the happiness and social order of society.

"Large towns, at this crisis of the country's history, ought to be specially looked to by the British Legislature; and we would recommend the above, as an instant and preliminary measure, to one that may prevade every parish in the land; at the same time, forming one great national system of intellectual and moral training.

"We must, however strange, talk as familiarly of millions for education as we were wont to do for war. And, if these sums are objected to for *preventing* crime and adding intelligence, comfort, and happiness to the mass of the working population, we ask such persons to reflect on the following amount expended for the punishment of crime:

Cost of Glasgow Jail £34,800
Ditto   Bridewell, which, from the rapid
    increase of crime, it is feared must soon be
    increased 27,000
Sums raised by subscription for a House of Refuge   10,500
Annual expense of Glasgow police establish-
    ment (1834) 14,000
Expense of London Police establishment for 1832   223,160

"This last alone reaches to the funded annual interest of eight millions sterling!!"

These were our sentiments in 1834, and we have found no reason to change, with the exception of a greatly increased necessity for such moral machinery. If such sums are required for four of the towns of Scotland, what must be required for the rest of the kingdom?—what for England?— what for London itself?

B.

We give a survey of four factories, viz., in 1845, which was conducted upon what we consider to be the most certain mode of arriving at the real state of education and intellectual culture, and on the truth of which the utmost reliance may be placed:—See page 73.

REPORT OF THE EXAMINATION OF 67 WORK-PEOPLE (BOYS AND GIRLS) AT A COTTON-SPINNING FACTORY, GLASGOW.

READING.	13 to 15 years.	15 to 21 yrs.&up.	Total.
Read pretty well	16	12	28
Read imperfectly, and without understanding	15	6	21
Read very imperfectly, and without understanding	9	1	10
Could not read	6	2	8
	46	21	67

WRITING.	13 to 15 years.	15 to 21 yrs.&up.	Total.
Wrote very imperfectly	9		18
Could not write	33	16	49
	42	25	67

SCRIPTURE HISTORY.	13 to 15 years.	15 to 21 yrs.&up.	Total.
Had a knowledge of a few of the leading events and characters in the Old and New Testaments	4	7	11
Had almost no knowledge of Scripture characters and events	28	14	42
Who had never heard of Jesus Christ but from the mouth of swearers	12	2	14
	44	23	67

Two answered that God was the first man. One said that the soul would die with the body; and one was ignorant of the resurrection, and refused to believe it.

Glasgow, January 11th, 1845.

REPORT OF THE EXAMINATION OF 229 WORK-PEOPLE (BOYS AND GIRLS) AT A WOOLLEN FACTORY, GLASGOW.

READING.	13 to 15 years.	15 to 21 yrs.&up.	Total.
Read pretty well	19	29	48
Read imperfectly, and without understanding	16	15	31
Read very imperfectly, and without understanding	18	23	41
Could not read	69	40	109
	122	107	229

WRITING.	13 to 15 years.	15 to 21 yrs.&up.	Total.
Wrote very imperfectly	15	26	41
Could not write	107	81	188
	122	107	229

SCRIPTURE HISTORY.	13 to 15 years.	15 to 21 yrs.&up.	Total.
Had a knowledge of a few of the leading characters in the Old and New Testaments	8	18	26
Had no knowledge of either the Old or New Testaments	105	77	182
Had never heard of Jesus Christ but from the mouth of swearers	9	12	21
	122	107	229

Four answered that God was the first man. One, that Jesus was the first man. One, that Eve was the first man. One, that Adam and Eve were saved at the flood. One, never heard of "heaven or hell." One, when asked about "heaven and hell," said, "she kent naething about thae things."

Glasgow, January 13th, 1845.

REPORT OF THE EXAMINATION OF 131 WORK-PEOPLE (BOYS AND GIRLS) IN A COTTON-SPINNING FACTORY.

READING.	13 to 15 years.	15 to 21 yrs.&up.	Total.
Read pretty well	36	12	48
Read imperfectly, without understanding	31	13	44
Could not read	35	4	39
	102	29	131

WRITING.	13 to 15 years.	15 to 21 yrs.&up.	Total.
Wrote tolerably	22	9	31
Wrote not at all	82	18	100
	104	27	131

GENERAL INFORMATION.	13 to 15 years.	15 to 21 yrs.&up.	Total.
Who had a little general information	42	17	59
Totally ignorant	61	11	72
	103	28	131

SCRIPTURE HISTORY, &c.	12 to 15 years.	15 to 21 yrs.&up.	Total.
Knew who Christ was, and had a very imperfect knowledge of any portion of Scripture history	82	23	105
Did not know who Jesus Christ was	21	5	26
	103	28	

Eight of the above children said God was the first man. One said Jesus was the Saviour of Christ. One said Eve was the first man. One said Moses was the Virgin Mary's wife. One said Christ was the first man. Two said Christ was the first man.

The manager of this factory takes a great interest in the education of the children; and by uniformly preferring such as can read to those who are unable to do so, has, within the last year, very materially improved the educational condition of the works.

Glasgow, January 16th, 1845.

REPORT OF THE EXAMINATION OF 271 WORK-PEOPLE EMPLOYED IN A COTTON STEAM-LOOM FACTORY, GLASGOW.

READING.	13 to 15 years.	15 to 21 yrs.&up.	Total.
Read pretty well	60	40	100
Read imperfectly, without understanding	35	22	57
Able only to spell short words..........	36	28	64
Could not read	37	13	50
	168	103	271

WRITING.	13 to 15 years.	15 to 21 yrs.&up.	Total.
Wrote tolerably..........	8	9	17
Could write a little	26	24	50
Could not write	134	70	204
	168	103	271

SCRIPTURE HISTORY.	13 to 15 years.	15 to 21 yrs.&up.	Total.
Knew the names of a few of the leading characters and events mentioned in Scripture	38	31	69
Knew who Jesus was, but totally ignorant of the events and characters mentioned in either the Old or New Testaments	84	53	137
Could not tell who Jesus was, and nearly all of them never heard of his name but as an oath ..	46	19	65
	168	103	271

The following are a few of the answers received, viz., nine, that God was the first man. About ninety did not know who was the first man. Eight never heard of heaven or hell. Two, that Christ was our first parent. Two, that Eve was the first man. Three, that David was the Son of God. One, that the soul would die with the body. One, that God was the Son of Jesus Christ. One, that God was the best man in the world. One, that Moses was the first man. One, that Eve was the mother of Jesus.

Glasgow, January 16th, 1845.

" This is a sad picture of the state of society in Glasgow, with its churches, schools, parochial and city missionaries, and a greater variety of philanthropic institutions for the improvement of the people than is to be found perhaps in any city of the United Kingdom, and proves that the Christian patriotism exhibited in benevolent efforts, parochial or private, has not yet applied those means by which the evil may be cured. Glasgow, except for a mere fraction of its population, is still without the antidote by which it can be morally and intellectually raised. We have moral machinery for the adult, but we have not for the young, during at least six days out of the seven. To *restore* is the aim kept in view, not to *prevent*.

" By these reports, out of 698 young men and women who were examined in the four factories, and drawn from all parts of the city and suburbs, 126 *never heard of the name of Jesus,* but from the mouth of profane swearers ; and of those who had heard of his name, very many were found entirely ignorant of his dignity, or character, or work. We are not to suppose that these young persons are Roman Catholics, for every person knows that whatever this class may be ignorant of, the name of Jesus is well remembered, and often repeated. The Roman Catholic children which were examined, very readily answered, that *Jesus is the second person of the blessed Trinity;* but when questioned as to their knowledge of some of the patriarchs, or prophets, or apostles, answers were given such as the following :—*Sir, we don't know anything about these gentlemen.*

" The young people attending these factories are far from being the lowest or most neglected of the population, and we apprehend these reports present a fair sample of the state of education among a large proportion of the working classes in the populous towns in the United kingdom.

" Out of 224, or one-third of the whole number who could read pretty well, very few indeed understood the meaning of the words they had read ; so that, for all the purposes of improvement, their reading could be of little service to them.

" In an ordinary statistical account of the extent of education, two-thirds of the whole number, at the least, would have been put down as *educated*, whereas, in actual fact, there was only a fractional part.

" These young persons were very particularly examined, during the month of January, 1845, by the rector and principal masters of the Normal seminary, assisted by a few of the older students and the foremen of each of the factories—in all eighteen persons. The examination was conducted by causing each young person, apart from the rest, to read a few verses of scripture narrative, after which they were questioned in the plainest and simplest manner possible.

" The four factories are situated in separate parts of the city and its suburbs, and in directions north, south, east, and west of the Cross. They were selected from others, simply because we knew that the proprietors took an interest in their work-people, and were willing to ascertain their real condition, both as to their capability of reading and their amount of knowledge.

" The proprietor of one of these factories engaged clergymen or missionaries to preach to his work-people one evening in the week, during a period of six or seven years, and established an evening class for a short period to teach those who could not read, or who read imperfectly ; also a library of interesting historical, moral, and religious books. His experience is as follows :—At the weekly lectures a large number attended at the first, but they gradually diminished, until none were found present to listen even to the most animated addresses, save a few of the pious and well-disposed who stood least in need of such instruction. Those for whom these lectures were principally intended did not, and would not attend. The frequent shiftings and changings of many of the workers in a town greatly conduce to this result.

" In regard to the evening class, teaching to read, although given almost gratis, presented no attraction to those ignorant young people, and the attendance was extremely limited and irregular. The library was neglected because it contained no novels or political books. In fact, this gentleman found all his efforts paralyzed, and is *shut up* to the conviction that whilst intellectual and moral cultivation *may be carried forward* to some slight extent in a factory, yet the elements of knowledge, and the habit of mental exercise, must be formed before the period when young persons may engage in a public work."

As a proof of the imperfect state of education, in a religious and intellectual point of view, and that this condition of the town population is not confined to one particular period of time, I shall state one fact I experienced in 1816. In December of that year, I opened what is termed a local Sabbath school, in which I first attempted to teach the young. Twenty-eight boys and girls, from nine to fourteen years of age, were collected from two small lanes, all of whom could read, and nearly all were possessed of Bibles. In order to have some proof of the extent of their religious knowledge, I took each aside on the opening of the school, and put the same questions to each. Who was the first man? Was there a first man? Did you ever hear of Adam and Eve being placed in the garden of Eden? Twenty-three out of the twenty-eight could not answer, and were perfectly ignorant of the introduction of sin into the world, and yet they could read and had Bibles, and might be stated to be religiously instructed !!! Up to the present day, I have met with similar exhibitions in different parts of the United Kingdom.

" A friend, who may be said to have trained himself since he left school (in 1824,) thus writes :—

" 'Your remarks on the distinction betwixt *training* and *teaching* or *telling*, reminds me that the teaching of my early school days did not even amount to telling. My first lesson in arithmetic was in this wise :—The master took my slate and keelivine, and jotting down several rows of figures, drew a line under them, and, returning the slate, told me that there was a count in addition. What addition was I did not know, he did not tell me, and, well I remember, I durst not ask him. The answer would have been a pinch of the ears. Sitting down beside a boy somewhat farther advanced, I inquired what the master wanted me to do? Put these figures together, said he—3 and 4 are 7, 7 and 3 are 10— put down 0 and carry 1 ; 1 and 6 are seven, &c., and so I wrought my way through my first exercise in addition, but the meaning of such words as subtraction and proportion I only learned long after leaving the parish school. Our lessons in religion formed the dreary work of the Saturday, when we fagged laboriously through the shorter catechism, without note or comment, or anything whatever but words—words—words, and kicks and cuffs when the memory halted and words were awanting. Times without number we repeated the catechism, from beginning to end, without the master ever attempting to explain its meaning. It was the same in reading the Bible or any other book. The Bible-scholar who was commended most, was the boy or girl who could work a tolerable passage through the list of names of ' those that sealed,' in the 10th chapter of Nehemiah; and, I remember it used to be somewhat a feat in school to spell ' Habakkuk' glibly in this fashion,—' An H and an A and a B and an A and a K and K and a U and a K !' One's memory is tenacious of what occurred in school days; but I cannot tax mine with a single instance in which the master (of a parochial school in a royal burgh) ever, even by accident, suggested *a thought* to the mind of his pupils.'

C.

The following may, in some measure, present the effects of moral and intellectual training; the one being more general and the other more particular.

A clergyman of the Church of England writes as follows, of date 25th March, 1844. "I am happy to say that the training system, introduced two years ago into my national school, has been attended with the best success. In reading, writing, and arithmetic, both slate and mental, the school will bear a comparison with ANY OTHER which I have seen. But there are some particulars in which the system appears to produce results, almost, I should think, peculiar to itself. I will select two or three of the most gratifying of these results in our own experience.

" MORAL EFFECTS.—During the whole of the last summer, we have no reason to suppose that, in any single instance, were any of the gooseberries, currants, or strawberries in our noble play-ground, taken by the children. The fruit, when ripe, was gathered and divided among them in the school-room.

" SCRIPTURAL KNOWLEDGE.—At the last public examination which I attended, the children showed an acute and accurate acquaintance with a large portion of the Old Testament, such as would have done credit to the candidates for ordination. They displayed, also, an intelligent acquaintance with the leading doctrines which are referred to in our Articles.

" GEOGRAPHY.—The knowledge conveyed to the children of the great outlines of this branch of knowledge, I consider to be perfect; by which I mean something very different from what is usually taken away from the more respectable schools in England.

" INTELLECTUAL HABITS.—As the understandings of the children are, under your system, continually *exercised* upon the subjects before them, it is utterly impossible but that they are acquiring a habit of intelligence that fits them for entering into any department of life into which they may be grafted. I can truly say, from what I have seen, that I would rather employ a mason, a carpenter, or a servant who had gone through this preparatory education, than any one who had merely passed in the ordinary routine.

" My impression is very strong, that you cannot confer a greater blessing upon the public than by preparing young men of intelligence and piety for the situation of masters in our national schools; selecting such young men of intelligence and piety from the church in whose service they would be employed.

" P.S. One hundred and forty-four children have entered this quarter; one hundred is the highest winter number, in old times.

" P.S. I have just inquired of the master, who corrects my statements by telling me that *one* was detected in taking a gooseberry. And I may add, that so perfect is the principle of moral training pursued in my school, that after the examination which lately took place, I was enabled to present to the children no fewer than ten pints of red and white currants, which they pulled and brought to me, and which had been permitted to ripen in their play-ground. A noble proof of the power of the training system."

Extract of a Letter from one of our former Students.

" Daily some of the children drop their halfpence* when at play. (Those who don't go home bring, as you are aware, their piece-money.) These are, as soon as found, invariably brought to me. The losers know where to apply and have their property restored, ' on its being proven.' This I consider a most important fact among children, to many of whom a halfpenny is of great value. Two or three halfpence have lain frequently on the table for eight or ten days un-touched. When unclaimed, they are given, by consent of the children in the gallery, either to the school library fund or to some charitable institution.

" A little girl came to me some weeks ago, saying she had lost her penny ; I was surprised that during the day no penny had been brought. Before dismission, I asked if any money had been found ? No answer. After much questioning, and a short lecture on the subject, I gave up the search. The following words were given to think of during the night. *Thou, God, seest me, and be sure your sin will find you out.* After prayer next morning, a lesson was given on the sub-ject. Towards the end of the lesson, I observed a troubled hesitating face in the gallery ; I asked them what they would think of the boy who had taken it, if he rose and came just now to return it ? ' That he is a good boy ;' ' that he is a bad boy ;' ' that he has done what is right,'—were the differ-ent answers given. ' Do you think that his coming and re-storing the penny makes him a bad boy ?' ' No, sir.' ' Well if he don't come, what is the difference ?' ' It makes him still worse, sir.' It is his duty then to *restore it.*

" Time will not permit to detail the process of the lesson, and the progress of opinion in the gallery. Suffice it to say, that after some time the guilty boy stood partially up. I asked him if he had anything to say. No answer. I asked him to come to me. He came and restored *a halfpenny*, as he had spent the other as soon as he had found the penny. Another difficulty presented itself. The little girl did not wish to make him pay the other halfpenny. About sixty— who happened to have a penny for their bread and milk— offered one of their halfpennies to the little girl, and vied

* Which they bring with them to pay for their roll and milk.

with each other in their solicitations to be allowed to give it. I gave him a halfpenny that he might complete the sum. He would have done it himself, I have no doubt, but he takes his luncheon at home and is allowed no money for bread. He since offered me a halfpenny in payment of his debt. Here was a triumph over a bad principle, which harsher means could never have so effectually secured."

A former student writes :—

"In the play-ground of this institution, notwithstanding that two hundred children daily amused themselves under no physical restraint, small fruit, such as strawberries and currants, were annually permitted to grow and ripen untouched. Some little rascals *from without* were the only depredators, and when a thief was occasionally seized in the act of stealing a flower or a berry, the master brought in the strange culprit before the gallery, which furnished a suitable text for a training lesson, the whole scholars sitting as judges. Teaching does not, and is not calculated to produce such results."

Another writes :—

"I might quote many opinions on the subject. One clergyman writing for a trainer for his parish, says, 'Our directors unanimously agree to the non-separation principle.' A former student, a trainer in one of the poor-law unions of England, copies the opinion of clerical visitors from his note-book as follows :—

" 'Another point for which you contend is, that boys and girls should be taught together. When I first came to this place, about three years and a half ago, I found the greatest prejudice existing against such a plan. I tried to point out the advantages of it, but all my efforts were fruitless for a period of fifteen months. At length they agreed to let them have the Bible-lesson in the morning together. It was followed by none of the evil consequences they anticipated; on the contrary, the happiest results were produced. They are now so convinced of its good effects, both upon boys and girls, that they wish them to have all their lessons together, except writing. I will give you the Chaplain's opinion of it. The following are extracts from his report-book :—

" 'Oct. 4.

" 'The improvement among the children continues. I find

that taking their lessons together excites among both boys and girls a most useful spirit of emulation, without any ill-will or rivalry whatever.

" July 29.

" ' Continue to perceive very useful results from the boys and girls taking their lessons in company.'

" ' He is not the only person who now approves of the plan. Several clergymen, who are guardians, think highly of it, and some of them have, I believe, adopted it in the schools connected with their own parishes.

" ' As to the effect the training system, as a whole, would have upon society, there can be no doubt but that it would be most beneficial. The effects it has upon a few schools, and upon the limited numbers who attend them, it would have upon many. It is found to answer the most sanguine expectations of its promoters where properly carried out. From thence it may be inferred that it would have the same effect upon all the schools in the empire, and upon all the youth thereof, did they attend them.

" ' I do not mean to say that crime would be at an end were training schools established throughout the length and breadth of the land, but I do say, that it would be diminished to a degree of which we have no conception.'

" Another student writes as follows :—

" ' I shall, for the present, confine myself chiefly to facts illustrative of its effects on the moral character of the children. The crowded state of the school is, perhaps, the best proof that can be given of its power *intellectually*. Inasmuch as parents generally look more to mere intellectual acquirement than to physical or moral or religious culture.

" ' The effects of physical training, or of the alternation of bodily and mental exercise, while manifested by the healthy and happy look of all generally, are especially visible in the case of delicate children. Many who have entered the school so feeble and languid in their habits as to be scarcely able to enter into any of the boys' amusements, are now as active and vigorous as their play-fellows. This change can only be known to the trainer and parents.

" ' Many of the poorer children enter with faces already saddened with the difficulties which press upon the parents, in others the hidden look of the villain begins to appear. A melancholy street-training has been going on in their case with fearful effect, to counteract the evil influences of which, the utmost watchfulness and diligence, on the part of the master, are necessary. It is deeply interesting to mark those saddened and harsher features gradually wearing away under the influence of play-ground intercourse with better trained boys, and to see the open artless look of boyhood assuming its proper place.

" ' EFFECTS MORALLY.—In the play-ground there are, under my own and assistants superintendents, every day, nearly two hundred children at play. During last summer and autumn there was not, with one exception, a single flower taken from the borders that surrounded the play-ground. For about a month after the commencement of each quarter, there is much trouble with new scholars quarrelling and fighting. One of the most remarkable features in the conduct of the boys in the play-ground, who have been trained for some time, is the general prevalence of good feeling. A circumstance at which strangers have frequently expressed their surprise, after spending some time in the play-ground.' "

D.

From Mrs. Ellis's New work, entitled Prevention better than Cure.

" It is an agreeable task, after dwelling so long upon the evils which society is vainly attempting to cure, to turn to some practical means of prevention; especially to such as have now been tested in their real value by the experience of many years. I shall point out these advantages more effectually, by inviting the attention of the reader to an admirable work, by Mr. Stow, on the ' Training system,' in which many important principles of moral improvement are clearly defined, and their practical working strikingly illustrated. In addition to this, I am unable to withhold my humble testimony to the importance of the system, as the only *practical* exemplification of direct moral training established upon sure principles which it has ever been my happiness to become acquainted with.

" My own observations, however, can only refer to impressions. In the hope of doing higher justice to to the system, I have asked for facts, and the reply has always been in accordance with Mr. Stow's own introduction to the subject of moral training, as described in his work, where he observes—' Were a stranger, on paying a transient visit to a family, the children of which exhibited such prompt obedience as to be directed by the parent by a nod or a look; and further, did they at table, and in their own conduct, act in such a manner as to prove themselves to have been under excellent training—were this stranger visitor to say to the mother, ' I am quite delighted with the conduct and polite manners of your family; pray, tell me how you manage? How do you get your children to be so obedient to yourself, and kind to one another ?' The prudent mother would say, " *Come and see*—come and live in my house, and what I cannot possibly make you understand by telling or explanation, you may fully understand by observing my course of training. Little quarrels occur in my family, as they do in others, but I endeavour to render them as unfrequent as possible. My children sometimes exhibit a disobedient disposition, but I check this by causing them *instantly to obey*. The manner *how*, I really cannot explain to you; I act according to circumstances. The results you see, but the process I cannot possibly tell. Live with me a month or two, and you may see a little. I must be offended, the fault must be committed, before I interfere; and then, should you be present, not as a stranger, but an inmate, you shall see how I endeavour to proceed. The tempers and dispositions of my children are varied, and the nature of the provocations or mutual misconceptions requires the utmost delicacy, on my part, more, indeed, than in my own strength I am capable of performing, but I do my best, and God has been pleased to bless my endeavours." The mother-trainer may again repeat, in answer to the visitor's request, ' *Come and see.*'

"This is precisely the answer that a judicious school-trainer would give to a visitor who desires him to explain how

G

he morally trains his scholars,—' *Come and see;* remain here a month or two, and I will show you how we proceed. My children do not always steal, or lie, or quarrel, or fight, or deceive, or exhibit the strong propensity of selfishness. These must be developed in likely circumstances, and are then met by what we endeavour to render suitable antidotes. These observations, of course, refer only to the manner, or the method applied to individual cases. The system, considered as a whole, comprehends some principles of general application, which cannot be too earnestly commended to the attention of the public. The impressions produced upon my own mind on first entering the establishment, where several hundreds of children are brought under the operation of the Training system was one not easily forgotten, and such as could not fail to be equally powerful with all who are earnestly and anxiously looking for the *reality* of moral education. It is not merely that the children are orderly,—many schools are orderly; but their simple, child-like, cheerful obedience, as frank and as willing as it is instantaneous, appears at first almost startling, in connection with the extreme mildness and gentleness of manner by which this obedience is called forth, leading the observer to doubt whether, in reality, obedience is not the most natural and agreeable thing in the world on the part of the young towards the more advanced in years – the ignorant towards the better instructed. Although men are chiefly employed as trainers, the kindness of their manner to the children could not be exceeded by that of the gentlest of mothers; and instead of those loud, harsh, hacking questions which, in some of our public schools, produce an effect like plucking the answer out of a child by main force, the questioning of these masters more resembles a system of calm inquiry, pursued in connection with the young and simple-hearted, for the especial purpose of eliciting truth. By this and many similar means a humanising effect is produced upon the children, so that while in masses of hundreds they are obedient, as if actuated by one impulse, to the slightest waving of an authoritative hand; they are towards each other, as well as towards their instructors, courteous and even polite, in their willingness to make selfish gratification give place to the higher considerations of justice and kindness.

" In the very heart of a city like Glasgow, the question naturally suggested itself to my mind—'What do you do with those vices which exhibit themselves so plentifully even in the rural districts of England, such as theft, for instance?' and the answer of Mr. Stow was then what it has since been, ' that the training system, when fully conducted, produces such an improved moral influence on *all* the children, that, although there are daily checks, and a constant moulding of character and habit required, it is seldom that any one can long resist the power of this natural and christian system. For there is, first, the restraining of the physical or outward habit; the infusion of christian, of course honourable and courteous conduct, on simple Bible principles; the eye of the master, and revision of the conduct in the presence of all the scholars; the eye and *sympathy* of the children themselves; which, all combined, seldom or ever fail in making the pilferer honest, the rough gentle, and the contentious less quarrelsome, even within a few weeks. These gradually and imperceptibly form into habits of thought, feeling, and outward conduct. In schools conducted on the training system, therefore, there are fewer cases apparent of vicious condect, except during the first few weeks, than in ordinary teaching schools. Ours is more a uniform or universal influence.' It is, as Mr. Stow elsewhere observes, strictly speaking, a system exemplifying the important truth, that ' prevention is better than cure.'

" The earnestness and simplicity with which the truths contained in this valuable work are described, are not less striking than their *practical* bearing upon the great subject of education. It is not peculiar to the training system that great principles are embodied in simple means. In physical science this has ever been the case, that the most valuable discoveries have been found the most simple, when clearly understood; and if we hail with a gratification proportioned to the utility of its results, that knowledge by which the miner is now enabled to work out his dark life in safety to its natural close—that discovery demands at least an equal welcome by which the whole human race may, under God's blessing, be assisted in walking in a path of virtuous integrity, benevolence, and usefulness, waiting only for the aid of His Spirit to give them a holier impulse, a loftier aim, a more enduring purpose, in their endeavours to act in all things consistently with his revealed and righteous will."

E.

The following appeared in one of the public Journals, and which exhibits, in some measure, the actual degree of the moral and christian improvement of the young men under the school trainers :—

" Junior Ward, Parkhurst, Isle of Wight,
Nov. 18, 1845.

" DEAR SIR, * * * * * *. The blessing of God has shown itself upon the training system in a most remarkable manner. The fostering care of our worthy chaplain, and the diligence and hearty activity of my assistant, to all human appearance, have been the means of turning many from darkness to light—from the power of sin to the service of God. Symptoms of a complete change in the general sympathizing of the boys have been apparent from the time the system has been more fully in operation ; but at last a flame has burst out, if not of religious fervour in all, certainly in some. This has extended through the whole of this part of the Establishment, so that those who remain in a hardened state dare not exhibit their malevolent propensities.

" About the beginning of this week I was much astonished at several of those whom we considered very good boys gather together in knots, and engaged in earnest conversation about something which they evidently did not wish us to know. Such knots and modes of conversation are, or rather used to be, highly dangerous in the prison, as they commonly ended in some deep-laid schemes of wickedness.

" Judging from the character of the boys, they were not molested, but considerable attention was paid to their proceedings, which, end how they would, were evidently of no common kind. On Thursday, one of the leaders asked me for a sheet of cartridge paper to write memoranda ; and as he is rather advanced, he is often employed to draw diagrams in an adjoining room.　At the eleven o'clock recess a number of boys as above went into the room.　I had quite forgotten the circumstance, and thought the boy was drawing some mechanical diagrams, when I was very respectfully solicited to step into the room.　And what do you think was there ?—a whole sheet filled with rules for a *society for the suppression of vice in the prison*—no ungrammatical jumble of crude ideas, but a set of most excellent rules which might have done honour to the ablest in the land, and signed by above twenty names. Room was left at the top for the Governor's name as Patron, our chaplain as President, and myself and assistant as Vice-Presidents.

" The enthusiasm of well-doing has arrived at a great pitch ; great numbers of boys exert themselves, and that too with no small success, in trying to reclaim those whose hearts are yet hardened.　My only fear is, that we shall be unable to retain it so high as it now is.　However, through the Divine blessing, we shall do our best.

" The blessing of God accompanying the *training* of these poor fellows, steeped to the lips in crime, has accomplished the effects which may indeed be expected wherever the training system is introduced.　Their moral condition has steadily risen and fallen according to the extent that the training system has been practised among them."

" Parkhurst Prison, Isle of Wight,
December 24, 1845.

" DEAR SIR, 　*　*　*　*　* 　You have already heard of a great moral change effected in the character and conduct of many of our boys.　It is very unlike a school of criminals. The conduct of the majority is most exemplary, and in many cases the evidence of evangelical conversion are of the most satisfactory kind.　I am almost daily holding spiritual conferences with individual boys, and my mind is often delighted whilst listening to their simple but unaffecting statements.　With tears trickling down their cheeks, they tell me of the burden of their sins, of their anxiety to be reconciled to God, and to walk in his commandments blameless ; whilst others are enabled to rejoice in a cheering hope that God for Christ's sake has blotted out their offences, and adopted them into his family. For a few weeks there was much excitement; much of this, I believe, was sympathetic only—of course it could not be expected to be permanent. It has subsided; but the good, *the real good*, has not gone with it. The boys delight in holy exercises, and are evidently as happy as they are good. We have no difficulty in conducting the duties of the school—it is quite a pleasure. It is not possible that I could have have had a situation more agreeable to my wishes and feeling. I doubt not but that, through the blessing of God, that the Bible-training lessons have come with power and divine influence to their hearts and consciences, and have been subservient in producing these most salutary effects."

This Moral Training School was visited by Her Majesty, the Queen, Prince Albert and suite, accompanied by Sir James Graham during the autumn of last year. Her Majesty expressed her high approbation of the conduct of the boys, and astonishment at their attainments in scripture and secular knowledge.

Having had occasion to visit London early in April last, I visited Parkhurst, and after a long examination found the reports fully confirmed; and being desirous of having the testimony of the worthy chaplain, I addressed a note to him on my return to Glasgow, expressing my wish to know the extent of what he considered real conversions, he being daily, occupied in holding private conversations with the boys. The following is the Rev. Gentleman's reply:

"Parkhurst, April 23, 1846.

" DEAR SIR,

" I should have replied to your letter sooner, but I have been more than usually occupied for the last day or two. It is with deep thankfulness to God for the work of His grace, that I express my opinion that several of the boys in the junior ward prison have been during the last eighteen months brought to sincere repentance, and have exhibited and do continue to exhibit by their entirely changed conduct the fruit of a lively faith in the Son of God. I use the word *several* instead of *many* of the boys, because my past experience in the ministry has made me more cautious and less sanguine; but I can add that of *many* I have good hope, but require a longer 'continuance in well-doing' before I dare speak of them confidently. ' Your system of imparting and *following up* by application) scriptural knowledge has been to these poor boys eminently useful. The blessing of God has indeed accomplished it, and I most sincerely hope that the day may not be far distant, when you may have in some degree a present reward for your valuable efforts in seeing your system of instruction adopted in all our parochial schools, and numbers GLADLY receiving that religious knowledge from which they have too frequently turned away with weariness and disgust, produced by the dry and injudicious method of teaching hitherto in general pursued. I remain,

My dear Sir,

Yours very truly,

THOMAS E. WELLBY.

The Rev. T. E. Wellby, chaplain of the prison alluded to, being about to remove to a parochial charge, these poor criminals, desirous of expressing their gratitude to their worthy pastor, spontaneously drew up and presented the following address:

" *To the Rev. Thomas Earle Wellby.*

" REVEREND SIR,

" We, the undersigned, having been for the last two years under your immediate ministry and care, and having been thoroughly impressed by your disinterested kindness towards us, both in a temporal and spiritual way, (and to some of whom you have been spiritually useful,) now tender our humble and fervent expressions of gratitude and esteem, hoping that you will receive them; assuring you, that your departure causes us much grief and sorrow, but still thankful to the Almighty God that he has enabled you to continue your ministry so long with us.

" We also assure you, that your memory will ever be cherished by us in whatever quarter of the world Providence shall see fit to place us; and that a place will ever be found in our prayers for your eternal welfare, and that God would bless your ministry to those over whom you may have charge.

" We beg leave to subscribe ourselves,

" Reverend Sir,

" Your humble and obedient Servants."

Signed by 166 of the boys,—forty were not permitted to sign, not having yet attained what is termed *the good mark*.

If this system of moral and intellectual school-training were introduced into every prison and penitentiary in the kingdom, under christian, well-trained masters, might we not hope for like glorious results?

Parish or district moral training schools are no doubt more costly than those simply for teaching with the one covered school-room; but with the well-trained master they are more than proportionately efficient. I shall state the cost of a few of the first twenty-four training schools which were established in Glasgow, ten or a dozen years ago,—I mean schools with a play-ground and a gallery suitable for conducting the training system.

	Infant.	Juvenile.	Cost, including Ground.
Chalmers' Street, St. John's Parish, with Female School of Industry—good sized play-ground	1	0	£1130
St. David's Parish Schools—play-ground rather small	1	1	2080
St. Enoch's Parish — play-grounds too small	1	1	1877

Anderston and St. Mark's Parish Schools—excellent full width of play-ground, but 15 to 20 feet too short	1 2	2050
* St. Luke's Parish School—play-ground 98 feet long, by 35 broad—10 feet too narrow	0 1	750
Gorbals—Infant play-ground excellent—Juvenile play-ground too small	1 1	1340
Partick Parish Schools—excellent play-grounds about 110 feet long by 43 wide	1 1	1020
Greenock — Highlanders' Training Academy—all the three play or training-grounds are very superior, being about 102 feet long, by 86 feet broad—cost, including ground	1 2	200

ONE MODE OF ERECTING MORAL TRAINING SCHOOLS IN THE CROWDED STREETS AND LANES OF A CITY.

The greatest barrier to the establishment of training schools in a large town is the extreme high price of ground for the *uncovered* school-room, or play-ground, and especially in the densest portions of them, where moral and intellectual training is most imperatively required.

Without a play-ground there cannot be moral training or a training-school. The question is, therefore, can this necessity be met by any substitute, even *although a limited number of pupils only* may be accommodated?

* This School is situated in a most destitute suburban district of Glasgow. We may give one example of its sad destitution. By a survey made in April, 1836, out of a population of about 2400, there were 592 children between the ages of 6 and 13 years, and only 29 at day-schools. The General Assembly's School Committee have handsomely voted an annual endowment of £30 to the teacher, in order to provide cheap education for this part of a destitute overgrown parish, containing 80,000 souls.

"Within four years after the establishment of this week-day training school in conjunction with Sabbath schools taught by the same individuals, the superintendent of police stated, and which was communicated to the teacher, by him unasked, that *the number of commitments at the police office in that district had been reduced two-thirds*. We may gather from this that Bible Training and Moral Training are THE CHEAPEST POLICE."

We shall suppose a site is procured in the line of a street or lane, 72 or 74 feet long, reaching backwards as far as possible, but say 100 feet—erect a building. If three stories, arch the ground-floor without glass windows, and from front to back this will form the play-ground, partly covered by the flat above of, say 100 feet long by 60 feet broad—12 of the site being occupied by the passage and staircase.

The second floor will form a school 60 feet long by 30 feet broad, with a small close room 10 or 10 feet square in front of the stairs.

The third story same as the second story and the play-ground. The roof nearly flat and paved with *asphalte*, and surrounded with high railings, forming on the top a small play-ground of 60 by 30 feet. If the open flat roof be not approved of, then add a fourth story, with arched open windows without glass, so that air may be admitted freely front and back. The water-closets may be placed at the sides of the stair, at each landing, and flowers in pots may be placed ou the flat roof, as a trial of honesty and a training to it.

Some such plan as this would render the establishment of training schools comparatively an easy matter in London and elsewhere, for at least a limited number of pupils. The lower school should be initiatory and the upper one for more advanced scholars. The initiatory may be for infants under six, or infants of from five to seven years of age, and the other for boys and girls above seven years of age; or, if the arrangement must be so, the one school and play-ground may be for boys, and the other for girls of any age.

www.ingramcontent.com/pod-product-compliance
Lightning Source LLC
Chambersburg PA
CBHW051416200326

41520CB00023B/7261